PRAISE FOR

LOVE MATTERS MORE

In the New Testament gospels, Jesus presents love as the ultimate end of a moral life. But like many Americans, I grew up in a tradition that granted "truth" co-primacy with love. We were told to make absolutely sure we held all the correct beliefs and that we needed to remind everyone who disagreed that they were wrong, wrong, wrong. Jared Byas has come along in the nick of time with a powerful book to help us dismantle these false constructs and liberate ourselves to love without constraint. Just as Jesus taught. *Love Matters More* is required reading for anyone who has ever felt they had to balance being correct with being loving.

> JONATHAN MERRITT, author of *Learning to Speak God from Scratch* and award-winning contributor to *The Atlantic*

I'm the kind of person for whom the term *biblical* carries a lot of baggage. But I'm also the kind of person who cares about matters of faith and who longs for a relationship with Jesus that doesn't make me feel like I'm a soldier in the Roman Empire. If you're like me, you'll find *Love Matters More* to be a cool breeze on a hot summer day, reminding you of why you fell in love with Jesus in the first place.

> MIKE McHARGUE, bestselling author of *You're a Miracle (and a Pain in the Ass)* and *Finding God in the Waves*

In *Love Matters More*, Jared Byas takes the discussion of love into the hard places of life. The brand of love Jesus embodies is indiscriminate, unconditional, sacrificial, and relentless—it's the kind of love that is the identifying attribute of those who follow Jesus. Jared puts this radical call to love on the table where it belongs and draws wisdom to help others from his own struggle to love. This book will challenge, rebuke, inspire, amuse, and leave readers rethinking their own relationships. We will be healthier and truer to Jesus, and the world will be a better place for others, if we read and take to heart this revolutionary call to love.

CAROLYN CUSTIS JAMES, author of *Half the Church: Recapturing God's Global Vision for Women* and *Malestrom: Manhood Swept into the Currents of a Changing World*

What an amazing book! Jared Byas uses a lot of complete sentences and punctuation, and it's relatively free of typos! It's also beautifully provocative. Jared brings his philosophical chops to cut through the clichés and show that "speaking the truth in love" is deeper, more interesting, and far more important than our tired notions of "truth" allow. A must-read for people who actually have to engage other people.

PETER ENNS, cohost of *The Bible for Normal People* podcast and author of *How the Bible Actually Works*

LOVE
MATTERS
MORE

LOVE
MATTERS
MORE

HOW FIGHTING TO BE RIGHT
KEEPS US FROM LOVING LIKE JESUS

JARED BYAS

ZONDERVAN
BOOKS

ZONDERVAN BOOKS

Love Matters More
Copyright © 2020 by Jared Byas

Requests for information should be addressed to:
Zondervan, *3900 Sparks Dr. SE, Grand Rapids, Michigan 49546*

Zondervan titles may be purchased in bulk for educational, business, fundraising, or sales promotional use. For information, please email SpecialMarkets@Zondervan.com.

ISBN 978-0-310-35863-3 (audio)

Library of Congress Cataloging-in-Publication Data

Names: Byas, Jared, 1984- author.
Title: Love matters more : how fighting to be right keeps us from loving like Jesus / Jared Byas.
Description: Grand Rapids, Michigan : Zondervan, [2020] | Includes bibliographical references. | Summary: "For years, Christians have argued, debated, and fought one another while 'speaking the truth in love,' yet we are no closer to the grace-filled life Jesus modeled. Biblical scholar and popular podcast host of The Bible for Normal People Jared Byas casts a new vision for the Christian life that's built not on certainty, but on the risk of love"—Provided by publisher.
Identifiers: LCCN 2020000398 (print) | LCCN 2020000399 (ebook) | ISBN 9780310358602 (trade paperback) | ISBN 9780310358626 (ebook)
Subjects: LCSH: Love—Religious aspects—Christianity. | Truth—Religious aspects—Christianity. | Jesus Christ—Example. | Christian life.
Classification: LCC BV4639 .B93 2020 (print) | LCC BV4639 (ebook) | DDC 241/.4—dc23
LC record available at https://lccn.loc.gov/2020000398
LC ebook record available at https://lccn.loc.gov/2020000399

Cover design: Thinkpen Design
Interior design: Kait Lamphere

Printed in the United States of America

20 21 22 23 24 25 26 27 28 29 30 /LSC/ 14 13 12 11 10 9 8 7 6 5 4 3 2 1

For my mom, Anita—
who puts people over ideas and often models
how love and forgiveness can overcome disagreements

CONTENTS

CHAPTER ONE

ONLY GOD KNOWS IT'S AN ELEPHANT

This book is for anyone who has ever felt they had to choose between truth and love. It's for anyone whose heart has told them the way of Jesus is standing up for *people*, but they've been taught that being faithful to Jesus is standing up for *truth*.

Pastor Richard got up out of his chair and began to pace around his office. "Do you understand, boys, that what you did on Sunday put a stumbling block in the way of someone's salvation?" He was speaking to me and my friend John. We were ten-year-old kids. He was "telling us the truth in love," he assured us, because that's what God wants Christians to do.

For those who have never been sent to the pastor's office— it's like being sent to the principal's office, except instead of detention, this guy could send you to hell for eternity. When my mom told me Pastor Richard wanted to talk to us, I was worried. I didn't know what he wanted to talk to us about.

Picture a small Southern Baptist church in the 1980s. There

are rows and rows of wooden pews with red, itchy cushions the same color and texture as the carpet on the floor. On the Sunday morning in question, I'd been sitting up against the straight, hard back of one of the pews, thinking that the original designer likely knew the people sitting in those pews would need help staying awake. Next to me was my best friend, John, whom I dragged to church most weeks, even though his family didn't attend.

If you've ever attended a Southern Baptist church service, you know that the climax is the altar call. If you haven't had the experience, the altar call is a brief time at the end of every Sunday service where the pastor makes an emotional plea for people to come forward, confess their sins, and get saved. Everything else in a service is just pregame commentary.

We were sitting about five rows back from the front on the left side, right next to the wooden "scoreboard" that got changed every week, telling us how many people attended and how much money we had given. The piano music had begun, and Pastor Richard had just said in his hushed and serious tone, "With every eye closed and every head bowed . . ." When. It. Happened.

John and I stood up and walked quietly out the side door to the bathroom.

Now, I don't remember if it was because I actually *did* have to go to the bathroom or if we were just bored. To be honest, it's hard to tell the difference when you're ten. I did know what Pastor Richard was going to say next—"If you're feeling par-ticularly emotional right now, this is the time to recognize your sinfulness and ask Jesus into your heart." I had that part down and had already asked Jesus into my heart at least five times by that point. So it seemed reasonable, what with every head bowed and every eye closed, that it would be a good time to take action.

A few days later, I learned about the summons. Not long after that, John and I were sitting on the couch in Pastor Richard's office.

"Boys, I want you to know that you're not in trouble," Pastor Richard began. "But I want to share something with you because I care about you." He then proceeded to shame us for getting up during the service at the altar call. It turns out we had probably caused at least a few souls to face eternal damnation because we distracted them from saying the Sinner's Prayer™ by getting up to go to the bathroom.

Even at age ten, I took my faith seriously. It was devastating to hear the pastor tell me I might have caused someone to go to hell because I went to the bathroom. I never felt any love from Pastor Richard, before or since, but I sure felt judged and shamed.

This is my first memory of a Christian trying to love me who clearly spent way more time learning *what* to believe than *how* to believe. I have heard my entire life that Christianity is about *love*, but what I saw—through our programs, services, and interactions—is that Christianity is about *belief*. I've come to realize that fear about being wrong in our beliefs has crowded out the clear message of Jesus' life and death—the unmistakable emphasis in the Bible and in thousands of years of church tradition—*love matters more.*

LOVE FEELS LIKE LOVE

When I was a pastor, I led a weekly class for atheists called For Skeptics Only. It was held during the service on the weeks when I wasn't preaching (I was one of five teaching pastors). It was a place for nonbelievers to go when their spouse and/or family wanted to attend church but they didn't want to sit in the service and strain their face from all the eye-rolling. It was a ten-week class where we went through all the common objections to Christianity and talked about them. Our goal was just to help people see that they could be atheists and express their doubts in the church and God wouldn't strike them down. It was a success. Over several years, we achieved zero strikedowns.

One time, a woman named Carol came in for the first session, and within thirty minutes she was in tears. We started the class with everyone sharing about why they were there. Most of them said it was because they didn't believe and were hoping to have a place to talk and avoid the service. But not Carol. She couldn't answer the question because she really wasn't sure why she was there. She said she thought she was a Christian. She had been a Christian her whole life. But lately she had questions—questions about evolution, about homosexuality, about why bad things happen to good people. And her family, in an effort to "speak the truth in love," told her she probably wasn't a Christian anymore and she should come to the class to get straightened out. She was thrown into a time of self-doubt. She was devastated.

Her family thought they were doing what was right. They had been taught that since people go to hell for believing the wrong things, the most loving thing they could do for Carol was tell her where she was getting it wrong and then provide the list of right things to believe.

There are two problems with this. First, the Bible doesn't say people go to hell for not believing the right things. The idea that when we die we're all going to sit down and be given a #2 pencil so we can fill in the "Heavenly SAT" is utterly foreign to the Bible. When Jesus speaks about punishment at all, it's reserved for religious people who judge (Matthew 7:1), religious people who force other people to obey a bunch of rules (Matthew 23:7), or religious people who say the right things but don't show up for people in need (Matthew 25). But secondly, telling people your opinion about their beliefs isn't the most loving thing you can do. On a list of the most loving things you can do for another human being, showering them with your enlightened opinion is probably around #138 on the list, right after regifting them a present you didn't want but have convinced yourself they will love.

The "truth telling" my friend in the class received didn't feel like love. There's a word for people telling you they love you while what you experience is actually only pain and loneliness: abuse. And doing it all in the name of truth doesn't change that.

Honest conversations about how we experience people or how we feel about others can be an important part of love, even crucial. But something is out of whack when I hear story after story of people being hurt by people who are "just telling the truth in love."

In both of my stories above, the people's intentions were good. Pastor Richard wanted me and John to know how important it is to bring people to Jesus. Carol's family wanted to make sure she ended up in heaven with them. Most of the time, people do genuinely think they are telling the truth in love. But there is a broken system at work. Too often we think we are being loving when we aren't. And one of the reasons for that broken system is that we've misunderstood the relationship between truth and love.

What do people mean by *love* when sharing something

hurts the person standing right in front of them? What do people mean by *truth* when there are so many different opinions out there about what it means to be Christian?

If we can't come up with better answers to those questions than the ones currently circulating, and if we can't come up with better ways of behaving with other human beings who don't think exactly like us, we can expect to see even more people (rightly) walk or, more accurately, limp away from Christian faith.

While the impulse to tell the truth in love often springs from a desire to help people avoid mistakes that may hurt them in the long run, our telling often adds control, discomfort, and fear into the mix, and the impulse gets turned upside down. The intention may be good, but it can easily become a sneaky way to tell people why they're wrong about their lives so we can feel more certain in our own positions and feel good about our own moral standing before God.

To figure this out, we need to start with the idea of *absolute truth*—the idea that we can know with certainty everything there is to know about the world. We need to create a new vision for the Christian life that is built not on the safety and certainty of our opinions but on the risk and uncertainty of love. We need to start there.

ONLY GOD KNOWS IT'S AN ELEPHANT

There is an ancient story about three blind men on a journey together, and each happens upon an object at almost the same time. One of the blind men bumps up against something that feels broad and round, like a tree trunk, and so he announces to the rest, "It's a tree trunk, y'all; carry on." The second blind man takes another step and is smacked in the face with something skinny, with a small tuft at the end. "It's not a tree trunk," he says. "It's a rope." The third blind man, wanting to settle things once and for all, puts his hand out and feels something very hard, broad, tall, and flat. "What are you guys talking about? You need to get your hands checked out by the doctor when we get back to the village. It's not a rope or a tree trunk; it's clearly just a wall."[1]

There are some good things about this story, including the overall point. The point of the story is that we should be humble about what we know. We are all a little blind, after all. We may all be experiencing the same thing, but from a different angle, with a different perspective. As one human being in a particular place and time, I know I will find it hard to know the whole story. This will be an important lesson to remember throughout this book.

However, there are also some problems with the story. Like, why are three blind men walking alone in a place where they might happen upon an elephant? What kind of sociopathic village are these men living in where three blind men can wander off into the jungle alone? Go with them for goodness' sake. But that's for another time. I have another nit to pick with this story.

The punch line of the story assumes that the person telling the story—and we, the reader of this story—knows it's an elephant!

The whole point is to put ourselves in the position of one of the blind men, and yet at the end, the thrust of the point hinges on us nodding and going, "Oh, I see. That was his leg, his tail, and his body. Those guys were limited, but we could see the whole thing." But if we were the blind men, we wouldn't ever know it's an elephant because we were only ever able to experience one part of the whole. What if in real life none of us know it's an elephant?

THE UMWELT

Speaking of wild animals, did you know Mariah Carey's highest-recorded frequency is 3,135 hertz, which she recorded on her 1991 hit "Emotions"? Stay with me here. I promise this connects. A dolphin can hear frequencies that top out at around 150,000 hertz. That means a dolphin can hear thousands of sounds we can't hear. Did you know buzzards can see a mouse from 15,000 feet in the air? Let me rephrase that for effect: a bird the size of a watermelon can spot a rodent the size of a lemon from *almost three miles away*.

Why do I tell you these things? First, because I wanted to pass on the joy I feel every day when I come home to four children screaming over top of each other to tell me their latest animal facts. You're welcome. But more important, these facts help us understand the world and our place in it.

Because of how their bodies are built, all of these animals see, hear, and feel the world very differently. The way the buzzard experiences the world will always be different from the way the dolphin experiences the world. The buzzard will see things the dolphin will never be able to see. The dolphin will be able to hear things the buzzard will never be able to hear. And that's true of almost every animal. In fact, this is so common among animals, scientists have come up with a word to help describe it: *umwelt* (pronounced **oom**-velt).

People who study animal behavior, called ethologists, came up with this word to describe the world as it is experienced by a particular organism. The world as it's seen, heard, and felt by a buzzard is its *umwelt*, and the world as it's experienced by a dolphin is its *umwelt*. In other words, there's the world *as it really exists out there* (what we might call reality), and then there is the world *as someone or something experiences it* (what we call an *umwelt*).

And these scientists, the ethologists, tell us those aren't the same thing. In other words, there is significant overlap between the world that dolphins experience and the world buzzards experience, but there is a significant distinction too. And neither one of them fully experiences the world *as it really exists out there*. They are always limited. Like the blind man who only feels the tail of the elephant, the dolphin will only ever experience reality through its *umwelt*.

It seems pretty obvious that the same is true for humans. In addition to our bodies being built differently, we also have different cultures, personalities, experiences, and even languages. We experienced this firsthand in 2015 with "The Dress,"[2] and then again in 2018 with "Laurel or Yanny."[3] (If you do not spend countless hours on the internet like some of the more sophisticated of us, take a minute to Google both of these cultural phenomena before returning to this book.) Many of us saw reality as blue, while many others saw reality as gold. Many of us heard Laurel, while many of us heard Yanny.

In many ways, we are limited by our senses. And our limitations cause us to explore the world differently than other people do. My nose doesn't work quite the same way as my neighbor's. When he smells licorice, it smells good; when I smell licorice, it smells awful. My ears don't work the same way as my wife's. When I hear my four-year-old son yelling for me at 2:00 a.m. because his pillow fell off his bed for the third time, my wife hears nothing. Not even a stir. *God forbid you just reach over your bed and pick up your own pillow two feet below you. I'd much rather wake up and walk the two flights of stairs and a hundred feet to get it for you.*

But it's not just our senses that limit how much of the world we can experience; it's also our ignorance. Think about how much we didn't know when we were seven years old. And how much we didn't know when we were eighteen. And thirty. And ten years from now, regardless of how old we are right now, our older self will probably think back on how much we didn't know ten years ago.

I was reminded of this last year when I told my kids I was going to London to speak at a conference. "Are you going to hang out with Harry Potter while you're there?" my six-year-old daughter asked with genuine hope. For a six-year-old, there are probably only about a hundred people who live in the world: friends, family, and people she sees on TV.

The world my kids occupy is smaller than mine. And the world I occupy is smaller than the whole world. As we get older, our world expands. We realize that we can be more than just nurses and fire truck drivers when we grow up. We understand that celebrities are hard to reach, and that there are more than a handful of actors sitting around waiting to make the next movie that comes out.

Every time we learn something new, we are essentially saying, *My world just got a little bigger and a little more aligned with reality.* And since I think we can agree that we can never learn everything there is to know about the world, every time you learn something new, you are admitting that *your world*, the world as you experience it, is smaller than *the world as it really is.*

You are admitting you have an *umwelt*—a particular way you experience the world. And just as children's worlds expand as they grow up, and just as the worlds of the blind men expanded, so our world expands as we learn more and more about it.

And that's the real problem. We all have our own *umwelt.* How do we know when we are right about the world? How do we know when our *umwelt* matches up with *reality* and when we are wrong? We already admitted we are all ignorant, learning new things every day. We all have times when we feel the elephant's trunk and truly believe it's a tree trunk.

SWANS AND ABSOLUTE TRUTH

To drive home the point even further, I introduce you to the Roman poet Juvenal. He wrote a popular collection of satirical poems in the early second century (sometime between the years 100 and 127 CE). He has this charming line in Satire VI: The Ways of Women: "Do you say no worthy wife is to be found among all these crowds? Well, let her be handsome, charming, rich and fertile; let her have ancient ancestors ranged about her halls; let her be more chaste than the disheveled Sabine maidens who stopped the war—a prodigy as rare upon the earth as a black swan! yet who could endure a wife that possessed all perfections?"[4]

In case you didn't understand, let me summarize: "A woman who is pretty, charming, rich, a virgin, and will bear me many

11

children? Impossible. Amirite? And even if she existed, wouldn't she be insufferable to be around? Amirite? I'm hilarious."

Someone get this man some bell hooks, stat!

Here in this poem we have the earliest written version of a popular saying: "*Rara avis in terris nigroque simillima cygno,*" or in English, "a prodigy as rare upon the earth as a black swan."

This phrase, or a shortened version of it, became very popular in medieval Europe to talk about something impossible. It is similar to us saying "when pigs fly" or "a cold day in hell." In other words, it ain't gonna happen. Why did this phrase represent an impossibility? Well, it was common knowledge back then that all swans were white. After all, all historical records indicated that swans were white, and all observable swans in Europe were white.

And then, on a fateful day in 1697, for Willem de Vlamingh, a Dutch explorer touring Western Australia, the impossible became possible. He and his crew observed black swans for the first time. In 1726, two of the birds were captured and brought to Europe as proof.[5]

For fourteen hundred years, "everybody knew" that swans were white, and only white. It was scientifically documented and so deeply cemented in the popular culture that it served as a common phrase to talk about what was impossible. What was thought to be absolute knowledge became in one moment false and irrelevant.

From then on, anyone who saw these black swans suddenly expanded their *umwelt*. In one moment, the world as they knew it changed from a world in which black swans were impossible to a world in which black swans were not just possible but right in front of them. No matter how much we expand our own experience of the world, we will never know everything. There will always be more black swans.[6]

So why have I paraded this Noah's ark of animal stories in front of you? It sounds simple, but it's so important for us to understand that we are limited. In other words, *we are not able to grasp absolute truth* or *reality as it really is.* Yet in certain parts of Christianity we have made absolute truth an idol, and God has been replaced. We are deeply afraid of what it means for us if humans do not have access to absolute truth. And that fear comes out in hurtful ways.

Here is what it means, by the way, if we do not have access to absolute truth: since we can only see our slice of the world, we can't rely solely on our own opinions but have to be humble and trust others, including God, for a fuller understanding of reality. *Hide your kids. Oh, the horror.*

In all my sojourns with pagans and atheists, I've never heard anyone deny that there is an absolute truth, only that humans, since the tower of Babel, have been too blinded by pride and fear to see how little access we have to it. And that same fear and pride have crept into Christianity, which has weaponized Paul's encouragement to "speak the truth in love" (see Ephesians 4:15).

If we don't solve the Christian culture's addiction to "truth," we may miss entirely what it means to love other people truly. Or as philosopher Brand Blanshard said way back in 1939, "If we can know fact only through the medium of our own ideas, the original forever eludes us."[7] That is to say, *maybe only God knows it's an elephant.*

That's it. It's really not that controversial.

So why do people idolize absolute truth? Why do people get so upset when you question it?

THE POSTMODERN BOOGEYMAN

Growing up, we've all had those boogeymen that our parents, and their preachers and teachers, warned us about. In the 1950s, it was Communism or rock and roll. In the '80s, it was, well, still Communism and rock and roll I suppose. In my Christian tradition growing up, there were many boogeymen—Harry Potter, the Power Rangers, rap music, and R-rated movies, to name a few. I was to avoid those at all costs, lest the Devil use them to tempt me away from the faith.

Another boogeyman that was black-listed in my tradition was a way of thinking called postmodernism. Here's what I was taught about postmoderns (who, by the way, hated that term):

- They hated God. [Narrator: they didn't.]
- They wanted to do away with absolute truth so they could get away with whatever their morally depraved little minds wanted to do. [Narrator: they didn't.]
- If you agreed with them, it was because you just wanted to be accepted by culture instead of fighting it like a good Christian.

John MacArthur's 2007 book, *The Truth War: Fighting for Certainty in an Age of Deception*, is a good example of this line of thinking.

But that wasn't true at all. Just like J. Walter Weatherman, the one-armed man in *Arrested Development*, there was no postmodern boogeyman; it was a fiction invented to scare impressionable youths like me into toeing the party line.

All these writers were saying is that unless you are God,

you don't know if it's an elephant. Unless you are God, you don't have access to absolute truth. We can only see it through our own lens. And, some of them added, it's pretty dangerous to others and the environment when we pretend to be God and have the absolute truth.

There is a great irony to all of this. While preachers and authors like MacArthur tell us the postmodern boogeymen are arrogant and prideful, feeling they can just dismiss the absolute truth of the Bible, I have experienced the opposite. It's interesting that those who do believe we can access absolute truth almost always also believe they are the ones who possess it.

We only have our *umwelt*. As we grow up, our *umwelt* is getting closer and closer to *reality*, but because of where we grew up, our personalities, how our bodies are built, we all have filters through which we see the world. And we can never take those filters off, because we are human.

ST. PAUL'S BLACK SWAN

Paul, that beloved apostle we assume knew everything, told us straight up that he didn't have access to absolute truth. He wrote, "For now we see in a mirror dimly, but then face to face; now I know in part, but then I will know fully just as I also have been fully known" (1 Corinthians 13:12 NASB).

But Paul wasn't always such a postmodern relativist. He used to have certainty about what he believed. In Philippians 3:4–6, he described how intellectually he knew his theology better than anyone; emotionally he was more zealous for the faith than anyone; and morally he was faultless.

He had it all figured out. Truth was the most important thing. Getting it right was what mattered most. And as often happens when people feel they have God figured out, when they believe getting people to understand the truth is the most important thing, Paul used violence to help convince people he was right, as we see at the end of Acts 7 and into the early verses of Acts 8. He approved of a public execution and then went from house to house and dragged people to prison who believed differently than he did.

Then Paul met his black swan. He had an experience that extended his *umwelt* and changed everything he thought he knew about God. Acts 9 tells the story:

> Meanwhile, Saul was still breathing out murderous threats against the Lord's disciples. He went to the high priest and asked him for letters to the synagogues in Damascus, so that if he found any there who belonged to the Way, whether men or women, he might take them as prisoners to Jerusalem. As he neared Damascus on his journey, suddenly a light from heaven flashed around him. He fell to the ground and heard a voice say to him, "Saul, Saul, why do you persecute me?"
>
> "Who are you, Lord?" Saul asked.
>
> "I am Jesus, whom you are persecuting," he replied. "Now get up and go into the city, and you will be told what you must do."
>
> *Acts 9:1–6*

His black swan so radically changed his perspective on what the world was really like that he changed his name, gave up his social status in the church of his day, and ended up giving his life for something that only a few years before he didn't believe.

Paul was staking other people's lives on the fact that he was right and others were wrong. And then Jesus showed up, and it changed everything. It was this Paul who reminds us that we can see reality, but it's always dimly and always partially. It was this Paul who ends his letter to the Romans with a doxology to the mystery of the divine. He spends eleven chapters trying to figure out how this whole Jesus thing works with Israel and comes to no conclusion. But rather than being in despair because he can't get all the details right, he breaks out in song:

> Oh, the depth of the riches of the wisdom and knowledge
> of God!
> How unsearchable his judgments,
> and his paths beyond tracing out!
> "Who has known the mind of the Lord?
> Or who has been his counselor?"
> "Who has ever given to God,
> that God should repay them?"
> For from him and through him and for him are all things.
> To him be the glory forever! Amen.
> *Romans 11:33–36*

It is this Paul's example that I follow that shows me there's enough truth to guide us but not enough to think there are no surprises left.

A lot of Christians at this point will say, "What about the Bible? Doesn't that give us access to absolute truth?" And to that we say, no. Remember, absolute truth is getting to know everything there is to know about the world. Bible or no Bible—sorry, darling—that won't ever be you because you have a small brain. Not you personally, of course. That frustration you are feeling right now—that's you finally recognizing your limitations as a human. Maybe in the future we will be able to build ourselves wings to fly and brains that can know everything there is to know about the world. But until that happens, we don't have access to absolute truth.

Now do you understand my gripe with the blind men and the elephant story? At the end of the day, the only real way to truly know, with 100 percent certainty, that our *umwelt* matches *reality* is to know everything there is to know in the world. We never know when the next Copernicus or Einstein might show up and show us we've been wrong about how the world works. Or maybe our story will be more like Paul's. His black swan wasn't Copernicus, but Jesus. A person whom Paul was certain was spouting religious heresies showed up after he died and asked, "Why are you persecuting me?" And Paul had to rethink everything.

And that's what faith is. It's not certainty in *what* we know; it's confidence in *who* we know. If we had absolute truth, we wouldn't need to have faith in God. In fact, we would be God.

FAITH IS NOT CERTAINTY IN WHAT WE KNOW; IT'S CONFIDENCE IN WHO WE KNOW.

JONATHAN EDWARDS WINE WITH A LITTLE HUMILITY

One thing that helped me in this journey was to recognize that certainty is a feeling. We are often on a spectrum of feelings—from feeling absolutely certain to feeling absolutely uncertain. These feelings are influenced by our interactions with the world every day. However, at the end of the day, our emotional life isn't the same thing as reality. We have seen again and again that at any point, a black swan can show up and disrupt everything we thought we knew.

In 2006, early in my seminary studies, I was invited to a symposium. A symposium is a fancy word for "meeting" that smart people use when they want to sound pretentious. It works. Next time you go to the local PTO, tell your friends you are going to an educational symposium and watch them fawn over your big brain.

This symposium was on certainty and was essentially a living room full of Presbyterians arguing back and forth about whether we could be certain about our beliefs in God or the Bible. After a few hours and a few dozen glasses of Jonathan Edwards wine (yes, that's a real thing), there were clearly two camps: those who felt we could be *certain* and those who felt we could only be *confident*.

To explain the difference, let's take a step back.

Have you ever felt certain about something but then been wrong? If you don't think so, put this book down and go ask your spouse. I'm sure they'll help jog your memory.

You noticed I used the words "felt certain." Think about it. Certainty and confidence are actually feelings. As your spouse can attest, just because you *feel* certain doesn't mean you're right. So then, essentially, even in those times when we feel the most right, we can be dead wrong.

Don't worry. It's not because you're broken; it's because you're human.

We can be uncertain and still believe in all kinds of things. Belief doesn't require certainty, just confidence. I believe all kinds of things I'm not certain about. I even act on my uncertain beliefs in really critical ways every day. For example, I believe that I won't die in a car wreck tomorrow. Now, I'm not certain about that belief. It could happen, after all. But I'll act on that belief tomorrow when I get in my car and drive to work.

The same is true about our beliefs in God or the Bible.

Honestly? It just requires four little words: "I could be wrong."

Say it with me: "I believe this thing. But I could be wrong."

For bonus points, also repeat after me: "You believe differently than me? You must not be a Christian." Just kidding. For real this time, repeat after me: "You believe differently than me? Let's grab some coffee sometime so you can help me understand more of where you're coming from."

And honestly, that's the heart of my story. I went from being terrified of being wrong to saying, "I could be wrong." I don't think that's selling my soul to the "postmodern culture." I think (but am not certain) it's called "learning humility."

If you feel you possess absolute truth, then this book is not for you. Unless you're God. Then, by all means, keep reading. (And if you're not too busy, I would appreciate a signed copy and an Amazon review.) But if not, then this journey with truth and love must begin and end in the willingness to admit we could be wrong. Or uncertain. Or mistaken about what the Bible really says about truth.

Throwing off the weight we often feel to "tell people the truth in love" will require that we realize our opinion is not the same as the truth. If I'm not willing to realize that "I could be wrong" about my own beliefs, then I can't expect others not to feel judged by my opinion. Without humility, there can be no love. And Paul says that without love, even if we speak the language of the angels (who presumably get more things right than we do), I'm just a clanging cymbal (1 Corinthians 13:1). In other words, all of our truth telling is just annoying noise without love, because love matters more.

CHAPTER TWO

TRUTH IS OVERWORKED AND UNDERPAID

Since we don't have access to absolute truth (only God does), I guess you know the barbarity of what our culture will turn into. There will be no morality; the age of the antichrist has been ushered in; and soon there will be more sex orgies on street corners than CVSes and your children will do marijuana before age ten. Basically, just watch *Mad Max: Fury Road* to see where we will end up, now that we realize we don't have access to absolute truth.

Oh, wait, that's just what I was told would happen.

Is it true that if we don't have access to absolute truth, we float hopelessly in a world of moral relativism where nothing is right or wrong and everything goes? No. Even Richard Rorty, the scariest of the postmodern pagans your pastor has warned you about, thinks that "anything goes" relativism is ridiculous. He says, "'Relativism' is the view that every belief on a certain topic, or perhaps about *any* topic, is as good as every other.

No one holds this view . . . If there were any relativists, they would of course be easy to refute."[1]

Relativism, the idea that right and wrong depend on the individual, sounds like something a perfectionist made up. We all have perfectionists in our lives, those Schmidts from *New Girl* who keep us from becoming lazy good-for-nothings but also annoy the heck out of us because everything has to be just right. For us, it's our oldest son, who's currently eleven. Ever notice it tends to be the firstborns? As my wife used to say to him, "Sorry, Augustine, you were the first pancake."[2] In any case, Augustine is a perfectionist. If his drawing isn't perfect, he crumples it up and tells us he's awful at drawing. The reality is that he draws better than I ever will, but from his perspective, it's all-or-nothing. If it's not perfect, it's not worth anything.

That's essentially what people mean when they say, "If we don't have access to absolute truth, then anything goes." In other words, if it's not perfect, it's not worth anything. Perfectionists are afraid that if we don't have access to absolute truth, we will need to crumple up the idea of truth and throw it out. But if you step out of this perfectionist mentality, you see how silly it is. As the philosopher Simon Blackburn writes in his book *On Truth*, "Everyday certainties do not require that we get the whole truth before we get any truth."[3]

In reality, we pursue absolute truth because we hope it will give us a sense of certainty and safety. If we know things absolutely, then there is no risk of being wrong. And that feels good. But that's not going to happen. Just because we really want unicorns to exist doesn't mean they do. Just because we want the Bible to explain everything about God and faith doesn't mean it does.

THREE DIFFERENT KINDS OF TRUTH

So let's settle for truth—with a small *t*.

Sure, we'll never likely get the whole truth about everything. But that doesn't mean we just take our ball and go home, pouting about how unfair life is. Our lives are filled with truths that we rely on every day. The problem is that some truths, especially some really important ones, aren't nearly as clean or clear as we wish they were. We have to work for them.

Each year, Merriam-Webster chooses a Word of the Year that seems to best sum up the year. In 2006, the Word of the Year was *truthiness*, which comedian Stephen Colbert had come up with. John Morse, Merriam-Webster's president in 2006, explained: "We're at a point where what constitutes truth is a question on a lot of people's minds, and truth has become up for grabs. 'Truthiness' is a playful way for us to think about a very important issue."[4]

So to channel my inner Pontius Pilate, "What is truth?"

Well, maybe the dictionary will help.

> truth [trooth]
>
> *noun, plural* truths
>
> 1. the true or actual state of a matter

The dictionary said it. That settles it.

Slowly raise hand
Teacher rolls eyes, sighs, and reluctantly points to me
   "But do we have access to what is 'actual'?
   "And what do we mean by 'actual' anyway?
   "And 'state'?"

"And 'matter'?"
"How would we know when we get to the actual
	state of a matter?"

As Algernon says in the Oscar Wilde play *The Importance
of Being Earnest*, "The truth is rarely pure and never simple."[5]
So true, Algy, so true.

Why is truth so complex? Well, for one thing, we try to
make the word *truth* mean too many things. To be honest,
truth is overworked and underpaid. We use that one word to
talk about lots of things that are actually different. It's like how
I talk about furniture. When I use the word *cabinet*, I mean
anything made of wood with doors or drawers that you put
things in. Of course, there are lots of more specific terms I
could use if I knew what I was talking about: bureau, dresser,
cabinet, or chest of drawers. Even now, I have no idea what
the difference between all those things are, or if there *is* any
difference. So many of us do the same with truth.

Sometimes when we are arguing about truth, we are using
the same word but are talking about very different things—
different *senses* of the same word. I want to talk about three of
these different senses:

- fact-truth
- meaning-truth
- wisdom-truth

Truth is actually shorthand for lots of things we lump
together. So if we want to do the hard work of finding truth,
we need to start here.

Fact-Truths: Truth If Everyone Were Dead

In 2017, Trump adviser Kellyanne Conway famously defended a statement made by press secretary Sean Spicer by stating that Spicer was giving "alternative facts." Chuck Todd, the interviewer, responded, "Look, alternative facts are not facts; they're falsehoods."[6]

The most basic understanding of truth that most people have is *facts*. Fact-truths are the objective conclusions we come to about physical reality. Or to be crass, facts are what would be true about the world even if everyone were dead. That is to say, facts are what exist "out there," independent of human interaction. The biggest question facing us when it comes to fact-truths is: How do a bunch of humans who are always influenced by their own *umwelt*, their own way of seeing the world, come to grasp things that are objective fact-truths about the world?

Well, to oversimplify and skip over a few hundred years of trial and error, we have come up with two answers: logical argument and the scientific method. Both of these seem to work pretty well. We have come up with a few dozen laws of logic and a process for how to interpret our experiences that allow us to keep our *umwelt* in check (rarely perfectly but always with an aim to get more and more objective). For example, the scientific method states that for something to be a fact, it must be replicable, falsifiable, precise, and parsimonious (begin with the simplest available theory).

These are the criteria used for any fact-truth, even though different fields have their own way of going about this process.

For the most part, the idea of "alternative facts" comes from three things: (1) we don't want to do the hard work of applying the laws of logic and the scientific method to what we are presented with; (2) we don't have the skills required to apply the laws of logic and the scientific method to what we are presented with; and (3) we are in political power and have very little accountability or motive for telling the truth because then our agenda would fall apart. There is very little we can do about #3, unfortunately, but we can work on #1 and #2.

Trust the Process™

The NASA website on global climate change begins with this statement: "Multiple studies published in peer-reviewed scientific journals show that 97 percent or more of actively publishing climate scientists agree*: Climate-warming trends over the past century are extremely likely due to human activities."

The asterisk takes you to this paragraph at the bottom:

*Technically, a "consensus" is a general agreement of opinion, but the scientific method steers us away from this to an objective framework. In science, facts or observations are explained by a hypothesis (a statement of a possible explanation for some natural phenomenon), which can then be tested and retested until it is refuted (or disproved).

As scientists gather more observations, they will build off one explanation and add details to complete the picture. Eventually, a group of hypotheses might be integrated and generalized into a scientific theory, a scientifically acceptable general principle or body of principles offered to explain phenomena.[7]

This is a great example of how flawed humans who do not have access to absolute truth have built a process that gets us pretty darn close. These paragraphs highlight the scaffolding we use to come to facts about the world:

1. Constant testing of assumptions and revisioning based on results.
2. Coherence into everything else we know.
3. Consensus of specialized experts.

In 2013, the Philadelphia 76ers (a basketball team, for all you non-sports fans) were terrible. For fans of the 76ers, that wasn't really surprising. But the team's general manager, Sam Hinkie, had an idea, a strategy.[8] Over time, this strategy became known among fans as The Process. And our mantra became *trust the process*. When we didn't understand why certain things were happening, when our intuition was counter to what the team was doing, we were told to *trust the process*.

When it comes to fact-truths, understanding what the world is like when we take out the human element, we can't just rely on our senses, intuitions, or experiences. We have to place those into a process that has been developed over the past few thousand years and then *trust the process*. And frankly, given that the scientific method has led to smartphones, laparoscopic and robot-assisted surgery, and a rise in life expectancy from thirty-five to eighty years, I would say we don't have much reason to mistrust it.[9] Since facts are the outcome of these processes, if we don't want to do the work to become experts in that process, we are often forced to trust the people who are.

However, there is a limit to the scientific method and logical reasoning. One reason for this is that there is more to reality than just what's "out there." We *are* humans, after all. And everyone *isn't* dead. We still have to live on this planet. So while laws of logic and the scientific method are great processes for coming to fact-truths, they don't necessarily answer questions of morality, religion, aesthetics, or what it means to experience life as a human being. They can answer how the world works independent of humans, but they can't answer the questions of *meaning* or *how to live well*. As Rabbi Jonathan Sacks says about religion, *"Science takes things apart to see how they work. Religion puts things together to see what they mean . . .* Science is about explanation. Religion is about meaning."[10]

Meaning-Truths: Sharing Human Truths

One of my favorite quotes comes from Neil Gaiman, who adapted it from G. K. Chesterton: "Fairy tales are more than true—not because they tell us the dragons exist, but because they tell us that dragons can be beaten."[11]

This quote states so perfectly the difference between fact-truths and meaning-truths. The scientific method would never produce a story where dragons exist—because they don't. But humans are more complex. We can understand that a dragon can *mean* something more than a dragon. It can be a stand-in for our fear, our hurdles, our challenges. So what is true? It is true both that dragons do not exist (fact-truth) and that our personal dragons can be beaten (meaning-truth). Both of these types of truth are crucial for us to navigate the world.

Just like *truth, meaning* can be confusing because it can mean so many different things. For our purposes, we are going to talk about meaning-truth as the relationship between something and someone (or two someones!) to establish relevance, significance, and value. In some ways, meaning-truths are about taking "the facts of life" (not the TV show, but the actual facts in our lives) and becoming aware of, or determining, their place in our lives.[12]

We all live in a physical world where facts are facts. However, we are all equipped with the tools to make meaning out of those facts. We all have the ability to become aware of, and actually shift, the relevance, significance, and value we place on our relationship to the physical world.

For example, imagine there is a three-car pileup, with three drivers involved.

> There are three wrecked cars. (fact-truth)
>
> **Person 1** drinks coffee each morning out of the same coffee mug, but it was dirty, so he decided to drink it out of a different mug the morning of the wreck. He's superstitious and believes he was in the wreck *because* of the mug. The relationship (the relevance, significance, and value) between him and the fact of his wreck is the meaning he attributes to it.
>
> **Person 2** has been saving up for ten years for that car and believes having a nice new sports car will get her friends, which is what she thinks she needs to stop feeling lonely.
>
> **Person 3** was in no hurry that morning, has adequate insurance to cover the damage, and tends to have an optimistic outlook on life. She leaves simply feeling grateful that no one was hurt.

While the facts stay the same, what the wreck means to each of these individuals is vastly different.

But What Do You Mean?

Things get a little more complicated when we stop talking about our relationships with inanimate objects or events and start talking about our relationships with other people. In that case, when we use the word *meaning*, we add an additional element. Now we must ask what the original communicator was *intending* to mean. In the example above, it would be absurd to ask, "What did the wreck *intend* to mean?"

But if we are talking about a song, a poem, or a book (like the Bible perhaps?), another person is added to the mix. And it's important that we respect their intentions and the relevance, significance, and value they place on the words they are using.

So when it comes to the Bible (or a song or poem or literature in general) and we ask, "What does it mean?" we are really asking two questions, not one. We are asking, "What did the person who originally put pen to paper intend to communicate?" first of all. But we are also asking, "What does this piece now mean to me or to my culture?"

We'll call these two questions "Intention" and "Significance."

When we ask someone, "What do you mean?" we are trying to understand *intentions*—what they are trying to communicate to us.

I have Mexican family members. They sometimes sneak Spanish words into the middle of an English sentence, and I have to ask, "What does that word mean?" When I ask this, I'm asking, "What did you intend to communicate with that word? What is your intention?"

But miscommunication, not understanding what another person means, still happens all the time.

Another extreme example can be seen in the generational

gap in communication. Imagine this conversation among a few teens in 2019:

TEEN 1: "Did you see her? She was clearly throwing shade."

TEEN 2: "Like I care; she's not even part of the squad. Bye, Felicia."

TEEN 1: "Someone's getting salty."

TEEN 2: "Obvs. That's me, Hundo P. TBH, when it comes to being salty, I'm probably the GOAT. You KNOW this."

If you were #blessed enough to witness this exchange, you might have to ask your teen daughter or son what a lot of these words mean. You would need to know the intended meaning in order for the words to carry significance for you. Otherwise you could easily dismiss it as babble, perhaps as conveying something not even true.

Communicating with the Bible

The tricky task of biblical interpretation is holding together these two senses of meaning-truth. Our relationship with the Bible is, like all relationships, a two-way street. We want to understand what the author was intending to communicate, and yet we also want it to communicate something significant to us and our communities of faith today. If we understand the intention but it doesn't communicate anything significant to us, it becomes irrelevant. If we make it significant without regard to the original intention, it becomes groundless.

I like to think of reading the Bible today as a "merging of horizons." Anytime something or someone collides with me,

I have to make it mean something and let it expand my view of the world. I have to take what's given to me and ask two questions: (1) What did the author intend to mean? and (2) What does it mean to me?

It's important that we don't unchain facts from meaning or meaning from facts. But it's just as important to remember that facts aren't the same thing as meaning.

It's also important that we don't unchain intention from significance or significance from intention. In many ways, meanings are the various conclusions we might draw from the facts. That is to say, we can't make things mean whatever we want them to mean. But that doesn't mean that things can only mean one thing.

For example, if you want to understand what the author of a book originally intended, you have to go ask the author. If you can't do that, you have to use a process that has been developed to get as close as possible. Research the author or person; study his or her life and work.

But even if you ask the author what they intended to communicate and they tell you, that's still not answering the question of what the book means to us as the readers. It's only answering the question of what the book meant to the author. The question of what any of this means to me personally, or to us as a community, is more subjective and can't just be decided by what someone else intended it to mean.

This task of respecting the author's intentions while also finding ways to integrate the Bible into my life in a way that is relevant, significant, and has value is messy. Like most relationships, it isn't bound by rules but by principles. It isn't bound by authority but by mutual respect. It isn't about right or wrong interpretations but about better or worse, helpful or unhelpful, a spectrum rather than a binary.

Even in the broader sense, some fact-truths are more open to multiple interpretations than others. Some fact-truths really do not lend themselves to a variety of interpretations. They do not have several meanings. Take the theory of gravity as an example. It really doesn't matter if you're a wealthy woman in Africa or a poor man in Italy. How we experience gravity will be pretty much identical, regardless of our *umwelt*. Gravity is very much in the fact-truth camp.

However, other truths really do lend themselves to a variety of interpretations. The most common example would be anything produced by humans: books, movies, music, poetry, speeches, etc. At the intersection between the intention of the persons who produced these works and the significance we find as those who consume these works are meaning-truths.

And in between, we have some very sticky situations, where it's hard to know if something is a fact-truth or a meaning-truth. In our public discourse, you can usually find these sticky situations when you hear debates on whether or not something is "socially constructed."[13]

Wisdom-Truth: Navigating Life Well

A popular saying goes like this: "Knowledge is knowing a tomato is a fruit, but wisdom is not putting it in a fruit salad." This third kind of truth—wisdom-truth—doesn't get talked about nearly enough in our culture, although it is the most-talked-about kind of truth in the history of thought, both Western and Eastern. I will argue it is the most important kind of truth for our everyday lives, in both Christian and non-Christian traditions. Wisdom-truth is that truth that has moved from our heads to our hearts and then out to our hands and feet. That is to say, wisdom is not beliefs in our head but a life well lived.

WISDOM IS NOT BELIEFS IN OUR HEAD BUT A LIFE WELL LIVED.

Here's another way of saying it: Fact-truths result in knowledge, and meaning-truths result in understanding. Wisdom-truths are about figuring out how to navigate the practical realities of what it means to be human. They're about applying what we know and understand about the world, ourselves, and others in a way that leads to a life well lived.

An Asaro tribe proverb goes, "Knowledge is only rumor until it lives in the bones."

But what is a life well lived?

Saint Augustine had some pretty wonderful things to say that have helped the Christian world go in the right direction for the past sixteen hundred–plus years. One piece of advice I've always loved is, "Let every good and true Christian understand that wherever truth may be found, it belongs to his Master; and while he recognizes and acknowledges the truth, even in their religious literature, let him reject the figments of superstition."[14] This comes from a chapter aptly named "No Help Is to Be Despised, Even Though It Comes from a Profane Source." Or, to give the popular paraphrase, "All truth is God's truth, no matter where we find it."

I say this to point out that many different wisdom traditions have a great deal to offer us about how to navigate life well. While all of us are hit with facts from time to time, each culture has taken these facts and developed meaning from them in diverse ways. And out of that come certain ways of being in the world that we call different "wisdom traditions." By wisdom-truth, I mean truths about how to navigate the world well. Each wisdom tradition, while similar, has its own conclusion for the question, "What is a life well lived?"

Buddhism, Sikhism, Stoicism, and my own Choctaw stories and legends are four traditions that come to mind.[15] I have over the years found wonderful nuggets of wisdom in each of these traditions.

- "You will never fulfill your destiny until you let go of the illusion of control."
- "When the path you walk always leads back to yourself, you never get anywhere."
- "Your mind is like this water, my friend. When it is agitated, it becomes difficult to see. But if you allow it to settle, the answer becomes clear."

These are all wonderful wisdom sayings from various traditions. Just kidding. These are all quotes from the tortoise Master Oogway in the animated movie *Kung Fu Panda*.

But seriously, there are thousands of wisdom sayings—sayings that share good advice about a life well lived but that also resist our urge to turn them into rules. Wisdom sayings often require us to live life for a while before we really understand what the saying is all about.

- "The fool doth think he is wise, but the wise man knows himself to be a fool."—William Shakespeare
- "Yesterday I was clever, so I wanted to change the world. Today I am wise, so I am changing myself."—Rumi
- "Humankind has not woven the web of life. We are but one thread within it. Whatever we do to the web, we do to ourselves. All things are bound together. All things connect."—Chief Seattle

FOXES, GRAPES, AND JESUS

A Fox once spied a beautiful bunch of ripe grapes hanging from a vine trained along the branches of a tree. The grapes seemed ready to burst with juice, and the Fox's mouth watered as he gazed longingly at them.

The bunch hung from a high branch, and the Fox had to jump for it. The first time he jumped he missed it by a long way. So he walked off a short distance and took a running leap at it, only to fall short once more. Again and again he tried, but in vain.

Now he sat down and looked at the grapes in disgust.

"What a fool I am," he said. "Here I am wearing myself out to get a bunch of sour grapes that are not worth gaping for."

And off he walked very, very scornfully.[16]

This is one of Aesop's fables, one of more than a hundred likely written by a slave and storyteller named Aesop in Greece in the fifth century BCE.

What are the fact-truths we find in this story?

- Foxes have been known to eat grapes.[17]
- Foxes do not speak in ancient Greek, Latin, or English.
- This was not a historical event observed and recorded by Aesop.

Fortunately, Aesop wasn't really interested in writing to provide fact-truths, but in telling stories that help us navigate the world well (wisdom-truth). So what do we do with the parable of the fox and the grapes?

Let's start with the meaning-truth question: What did Aesop *intend* when he wrote it? Aesop's meaning was explicit—he put it at the bottom of the story: *There are many who pretend to despise and belittle that which is beyond their reach.* However, as the story has been passed down through the generations, some have taken it to mean other things that were more *significant* to them.

Gustave Doré, who illustrated the 1870 French edition of *Aesop's Fables*, had a more specific and explicit meaning he took from the parable: *Some boys put down girls who won't have sex with them, saying they are sexually immature and only fit for sexually immature boys.* This meaning is possible because the French translator, Jean de La Fontaine, translated "sour" as "unripe" in French, which also means "sexually immature." Then there's Jon Elster, a Norwegian social scientist, who takes the parable as an example of a strategy for how we reduce the cognitive dissonance between desire and the inability to have what we desire.[18]

Interestingly enough, the different meanings people have

taken from this parable can have an almost opposite impact. For some, the fox is a trickster, and the moral of the story— its wisdom-truth—is negative: *Do not be like the fox, who unfairly resents the grape for the world not working out in his favor.* For others, the fox is cunning, and the moral of the story—its wisdom-truth—is positive: *Be like the fox, who has figured out a way to be happy in the world by finding fault in what he covets.* The fox has convinced himself that "everything happens for a reason," and so there must be a reason he didn't get the grapes.

These are *all true*, depending on what perspective you take. Not true in the fact-truth sense, but in the meaning-truth sense and in the wisdom-truth sense when the significance is lived well.

Are there many who pretend to belittle that which is beyond their reach? Yes. Are there boys who put down girls who reject their sexual advances? Duh. Those are meaning-truths about the world that map onto this story. But what is the wisdom-truth we can glean from this story beyond just what the facts are or what it might mean?

Wisdom comes when we enact these different meanings under the *right circumstance* and at the *right time* and in the *right way*. Sometimes we will navigate the world better if we read the story as an indictment of our childish resentment and escape from taking responsibility for our own shortcomings. Sometimes we will navigate the world better if we believe that sometimes not getting what we want is a blessing in disguise. Should we put down girls who reject our sexual advances? No. Should we belittle that which is beyond our reach? No. Wisdom is taking these meanings and then living well.

Aesop's parables show us that great wisdom-truths can be had without facts about the real world and with ambiguous meaning-truths. Some eighteen hundred years ago, the writer Philostratus was already praising Aesop for this gift:

> He made use of humble incidents to teach great truths, and after serving up a story he adds to it the advice to do a thing or not to do it. Then, too, he was really more attached to truth than the poets are; for the latter do violence to their own stories in order to make them probable; but he by announcing a story which everyone knows not to be true, told the truth by the very fact that he did not claim to be relating real events.[19]

As we mentioned before, fact-truths are guided by laws of logic and the scientific method. And meaning-truth is guided by intention and significance. But what about wisdom-truth? What allows us to say yes or no to certain definitions of a life well lived?

These definitions are often guided by culture and personal experience. It's helpful to ask ourselves, as followers of the Christian tradition, how might we define this wisdom-truth? What is our standard? What makes the Christian tradition distinct from Buddhism or Stoicism? I know I run the risk of oversimplifying here, but let me offer a definition: *a nuanced life of love patterned after Jesus.*

This is a crucial definition because this is where we bridge the gap between truth and love. This is where we learn why love matters more than fighting to be right all the time. The Christian understanding of wisdom is where truth and love put down their weapons and not only become friends but become the same thing. The highest form of truth is a life of love. All other forms of truth—fact-truth and meaning-truth—are subservient to wisdom-truth. And all wisdom-truth leads to a life of love patterned after Jesus.

There is a progression here: Fact-truth is what would be true even if everyone were dead. Meaning-truth is a spark of connection—intention and significance—between ourselves and others (the world, another person, a book). And wisdom-truth is thoroughly personal, meaning it cannot be true if you were dead, because it is a question of whether you—yes, you right there—are living the truth well. In the Christian tradition, that question is more specifically asked: Are you, right now, living a nuanced life of love patterned after Jesus?

Let's look at each of these words in a little more detail.

Nuanced. We don't have to go very far to find the need for nuance in the Bible. Take, for example, Proverbs 26:4–5:

> Do not answer a fool according to his folly,
>   or you yourself will be just like him.
> Answer a fool according to his folly,
>   or he will be wise in his own eyes.

So which is it? Do we answer a fool or do we not answer a fool? It can't be both. The Bible, as a book of wisdom, will answer again and again, "It depends."[20] As a wisdom book, the Bible is rarely giving us moral certainties or a set of rules or laws. It doesn't tell us what to think but provides questions and thoughts for us to grow our own moral muscle.

Lest we think this is just a point made in the Old Testament, please note that Jesus asked 307 questions in the Bible. He is asked 183, and he directly answers three.[21] It's almost as if Jesus wasn't interested in giving us answers as much as he was in making us "as shrewd as snakes and as innocent as doves" (Matthew 10:16)—that is, growing us into people who can make a nuanced decision based on a wise reading of the circumstances.

The basic premise of Gary Chapman's wildly popular book *The Five Love Languages* is that because we are all built differently, we can't assume that what we think will be loving will actually be received as loving. While Chapman outlines five specific ways we experience love, I have found his overall principle to be the most helpful: it takes wisdom, it takes informed nuance, to know how to love people well. If giving love in some sense depends on how someone will receive my love, it takes time and effort to make sure my words and actions will be *taken* as loving.

This is why any form of Christianity that sells certainty is a ruse, a get-rich-quick scheme that robs us of wisdom and courage. That form of Christianity tells us there is a black-and-white way to love people well, without the messiness of true relationship. In the same way that doctors are learning how to administer medicine in nuanced and specific ways to treat our physical ailments, we have to learn how to administer love in nuanced and specific ways to treat our spiritual and relational ailments.

Life. For the Christian tradition, wisdom is not about words but about existence and how we actually live in the world. We see this prominently in John's writings in the Bible. John sums it up nicely in 1 John 3:18: "Dear children, let us not love with words or speech but with actions and in truth." Or as the writer

Søren Kierkegaard says, "Christianity entered into the world not to be understood but to be existed in."[22] To be even pithier, Christianity focuses on the fruits, not the roots.

Love. Yes, wisdom is nuanced. Yes, it is to be lived, and lived well. But in the Christian tradition, the climax of the life of wisdom is the life of love. Whatever else it is in the Christian tradition, if it is not loving, it is not true, nor is it wise. So we ask, "What is love?"

When I was sixteen years old, I saw an older gentleman in a wheelchair trying to make his way through a local park on his way home. One of his legs had been amputated, and he was using his other leg to push himself slowly along. After driving by him, I decided to turn around and ask him if he needed help getting to where he needed to go. When I finally caught up to him and asked if he would like some help, he looked at me, completely annoyed, and said, "I'm not going anywhere. I'm at the park to exercise."

Of course, at first I was deeply embarrassed and defensive. *What a jerk!* I thought to myself as I sulked back to my car. But after I got over myself, this experience became an extremely valuable lesson to me: love is more than just intention or feeling, and it takes work to love well.

Bell hooks's definition of love (which she borrowed from M. Scott Peck) is helpful here: "the will to extend one's self for the purpose of nurturing one's own or another's spiritual growth."[23] How do you extend yourself to nurture your own and other people's spiritual growth? After all, I think we could make that definition mean whatever we want. It takes wisdom to love well. It takes time and energy to develop the skills we need. In other words, love is more than a feeling, and it's more than an intention (though it's not usually less). It takes action that considers how it will be received. Or as bell hooks says, "To truly love we must learn to mix various ingredients—care, affection, recognition, respect, commitment, and trust, as well as honest and open communication."[24]

This kind of love is what I call *true love*.

Rather than a group of people "speaking the truth in love," Christians need to be a people who express and embody true love. In the phrase "speaking the truth in love," the emphasis is on the *truth*, and *love* just describes how we truth-tell. But in the phrase "true love," the emphasis is on *love*, and *true* just describes how we love. Simply by changing the noun into the adjective, we have altered the course of the Christian life. The emphasis must always fall on acts of love, with truth girding up those acts of love. Instead, too often we allow the emphasis to fall on the acts of truth telling and miss the point.

Patterned after Jesus. As Christians, what we mean by wisdom and love is shaped by Jesus. When writing to the Corinthians, Paul uses a lot of wisdom language. According to him, there is something undeniably Christ-shaped about the life of wisdom that he feels God is calling us to. In fact, in 1 Corinthians 1:30, Paul writes that Jesus *has become for us* the wisdom of God. Or as Cynthia Bourgeault summarizes about Jesus, "He was not only a teacher of wisdom, he was a master of wisdom."[25]

And what does Jesus' wisdom look like? Well, if the definition of love is "the will to extend one's self for the purpose of nurturing one's own or another's spiritual growth," then Jesus' wisdom looks like love.[26]

Speaking the truth in love looks very different if you live

your life pursuing wisdom rather than making sure you get the facts right. Does this mean that facts don't matter? Of course they do. I would like us to resist jumping on the perfectionist bandwagon. It's not all or nothing. We all live with facts. The question is: How might we go beyond the facts to find love? Can we let go of the white-knuckled grip we have on life long enough to see that getting our facts right about the Bible, about politics, about our neighbor's bad behavior, isn't leading us toward love?

CHAPTER THREE

BEWARE OF FALLING IN LOVE WITH COWS

O ne night when I was seventeen, I came home from a night out with friends and went straight to the kitchen to grab a bite to eat. Even though our kitchen was small, it was where we had our washer and dryer and our dining table that sat in front of a large window. As I walked into the kitchen from the living room, I could see my mom sitting there, working on something.

We began talking about the night, which somehow led into a conversation about Christianity. Well, to be honest, I tried to steer most of my conversations into conversations about Christianity. We were debating the idea of predestination—whether God chooses which people will go to heaven or whether we have free will. I had recently been introduced to theology, and after reading two or three books on the topic, I was clearly an expert and needed to change everyone's mind to save them from their ignorant ways.

"Aha, but you see," I said to my mom as I pointed a finger in her face, "you've just contradicted yourself." In an instant, she had grabbed my throat with one hand and my shirt with the other and slammed me into our back door. Our eyes grew wide as the realization of what just happened sank in. We both began to shake, and tears streamed down our faces as we sat in silence. Finally, my mom apologized as she explained that people pointing fingers at her was a trigger from when she was a girl and her father would name-call the children while pointing his finger at them.

That's the night I learned that getting theology right wasn't all there was to Christian faith. Knowing facts wasn't enough to bring about the kingdom of God I was seeking. It wasn't enough to conjure up love between two people or heal old wounds. That night, I learned a valuable truth: there's more to truth than facts—especially when you're a Christian.

That night changed me in ways I'm still learning from. It didn't change me right away, but it put cracks in my foundation. *Is the life of faith about being right? Is it important to make sure others get it right? Or is this about loving people no matter what?* For some reason, in my mind, those were very hard things to do at the same time.

From what I gathered as a kid, telling the truth in love was about telling the truth and *hopefully* doing so in a loving way. The emphasis was always on truth telling and not on love. And as I've gotten older, and hopefully wiser, I see that this should be the other way around. The emphasis should always be on love, not truth telling. The priority in the New Testament, as we will see, is always love.

We will see that in the Bible there is no tension between truth and love, because the highest form of truth is wisdom, and the highest form of wisdom is love. Did you get that? We will see that, according to the Bible, truth *is* love; there is no distinction. Jesus is about the way we live our lives and not the facts in our heads. We can't escape the conclusion that the priority of truth isn't facts, and it isn't meaning, and it's not even wisdom, but it's about love.

So when Paul says in Ephesians 4:15 that we should be "speaking the truth in love," I understand this to mean that if you're not *in love* with the person standing in front of you—acting in loving ways toward them—then you're not telling the truth, no matter what comes out of your mouth.

And so in a brilliant move, the Christian tradition moves us from resting on facts to actively finding meaning that propels us into a life of wisdom, which finds its ultimate fulfillment in love. The New Testament (as we'll see throughout the rest of this book) takes us again and again back to love—a love that is not over against facts. It isn't in tension with meaning or wisdom. It is a vision for life that utilizes facts, meaning, and wisdom in service to love. It is a lifestyle that integrates them all.

This is crucial to understand, because for the past four hundred years, many of us have gotten it wrong.

THE VENDING MACHINE THEORY

I firmly believe modern American culture has bought into what I call the "vending machine theory" about facts. This is the belief that the world will be made right when we get all the facts straight. The *real* problem with the world, this theory says, is we just don't *know* enough. If we could just get the quarter in the machine and push the right buttons, we'll get the snack (a better world) every time. It's mechanical.

To be fair, we've come by this idea honestly. Ever since René Descartes embarked on his journey to find certainty some four hundred years ago with his famous saying, "I think, therefore I am," Western culture has become more and more focused on the facts.

We have spent four hundred years putting an increasing emphasis on getting all the facts about the universe right and not nearly enough time cultivating the skills to create better meaning, more wisdom, and a life of love.

One example is the explosion of STEM programs (science, technology, engineering, and mathematics) in the United States. The Department of Education recently touted that it surpassed President Trump's directive to invest $200 million in STEM education, announcing that in 2018 that number was $279 million.[1] Listen to the language around why STEM is so important: "There is no doubt that to advance our economy and our society we need to create the next great technology innovations, not just consume them. That's why there is such urgency for the U.S. to develop a stronger workforce of experts in science, technology, engineering, and math (STEM) . . . STEM-related disciplines are responsible for many of the societal innovations that make our world better."[2]

In other words, we have an urgent need to develop expert workers in STEM fields because our progress in knowing more about science, technology, engineering, and mathematics is what will make our world better.

However, we don't have to look any further than the ethical ambiguity surrounding the development of the atomic bomb to see that STEM isn't the *only* thing we need to make the world better. In the 1950s, we wrestled as a country with the implications of the atomic bomb. We were sure that science would bring Utopia, when it actually brought death and destruction.

What about an emphasis on subjects like self-awareness, compassion, empathy, civility, respect, peace, and justice?

Why are we surprised that when we put factfinding ahead of love pursuing, we don't end up with more love? While we admit that the world is made better by a recipe of equal parts love and truth, in my tradition getting the facts right was often more important than how people feel. In fact, it was usually said that giving people the facts is the most loving thing we can do. But if we have factfinding at the helm without a moral compass, facts can bring destruction just as quickly as they can bring peace. Of course we need STEM. Of course we need to continue to pursue facts. They have truly brought an amazing amount of good into the world. We just have to make sure that "speaking the truth" doesn't become an end in itself.

Most scientists I talk to agree. When modern-day scientists are asked why climate change matters, why depletion of natural resources matters, or why cancer research matters, they tend to fall back on something other than truth. Many of them fall back on love.

And so it should be in the Christian faith. We need to tear down the idol of facts about our faith, of getting our theology right, and shed light on our hypocrisy. We need to emphasize love and let it steer us toward a better world.

TRUTH IS A TOOL

Even though both my parents were born in Oklahoma to lower-class families, they were two very different people. My mom is Choctaw, which is a Native American tribe that traces its home to the southeastern United States. Her people were tricked multiple times by others in power, and she expressed this trauma by telling me explicitly not to trust anyone. My dad was a cowboy who grew up in a small Texas town and loved and trusted people openly.

They also grew up in two different religious systems. My maternal grandmother was an ordained charismatic preacher who lived in a van and traveled around, ministering to women. My dad grew up Southern Baptist. I was intentionally brought up in two different Christian systems. I was given two paths for what it means to be the "best Christian." For charismatics, the medal for best Christian was given to those who could show their emotions toward Jesus most emphatically. For Southern Baptists, the medal for best Christian was given to those who could memorize the most Bible verses.

Of course, this was never explicitly said, but it was communicated clearly nonetheless. Sure, there were a lot of other things both sides agreed on that we should be doing (destroy all your Jay-Z CDs and listen only to DC Talk and Newsboys) and not doing ("Don't cuss, drink, or chew, or go with girls who do" was a common Texas refrain). But overall, two paths were laid out for me. And since I grew up in both, I naturally put them together. Based on how Sunday school classes were set up, how I saw other adults behave in church, and what I was reading, showing emotions toward Jesus and memorizing Bible verses seemed like the best ways to make it to the top of the Christian food chain.

As someone who lives in the head and has a hard time connecting with emotions, I am grateful for my charismatic upbringing. As a professor friend of mine and I used to joke,

"Hey, let's go out soon to drink and think about our feelings." But it was inevitable that I would eventually choose more and more intellectual versions of Christianity. Being a Southern Baptist was a gateway drug to becoming a Presbyterian in high school—the mecca (not to mix metaphors . . . or religions?) of "faith built on knowing" stuff.

Lots of congratulations came my way when we had "sword drills" and I was the first to find a particular verse. I was asked to get up and teach classes based on how many times I interrupted a discussion with, "Well, actually . . ." and corrected either other students or teachers on their views. It was a glorious time to be alive.

So believe me when I say it was a hard pill to swallow when I started coming to the realization that Christianity is about living a life of love and not just a black-and-white life of getting facts right. I started to come across verses like 2 Peter 1:5–8: "For this very reason, make every effort to add to your faith goodness; and to goodness, knowledge; and to knowledge, self-control; and to self-control, perseverance; and to perseverance, godliness; and to godliness, mutual affection; and to mutual affection, love."

Peter is charting a course, laying out a blueprint, that begins with faith and ends with love. The rest are just steps along the way. As we all know, every piece of IKEA furniture has at least twenty-three steps. When we base our Christian life on how much we know, it's like building an IKEA bookshelf and stopping at step 2. It's not that knowing facts is bad or unhelpful. It's not that understanding what things mean, or even creating new meanings, is wrong. Those are also crucial. They are just stopping short of the end goal. They are building a life that mirrors a shoddily constructed IKEA bookshelf that works for a while and seems sturdy but eventually will be unsafe for people to be around.

Based on my personality (Enneagram 8 represent, y'all) and how I was trained in the church, I would be much more comfortable if the list were to read this way: "For this very reason, make every effort to add to your faith goodness; and to goodness, knowledge; and to knowledge, more knowledge; and to more knowledge, even more knowledge; and to even more knowledge, mastery of the Bible; and to mastery of the Bible, control; and to control, teaching everyone else the Bible as you use your superior intellect."

As ridiculous as that sounds, even as I look at it now, I'm like, *Yeah, that was pretty much what I was hoping for out of the Christian life.*

But if we chew on Peter's original list for a minute, we see something important. Knowledge is just a stepping-stone to other, presumably more important, qualities. And what is the climactic quality on this list? Love. We often think of truth and love as the two horses that pull us along in our wagon of Christian faith. They are equals that are both heading in the same direction. But this isn't the picture painted by 2 Peter, and as we'll see in the rest of this book, it isn't painted this way in much of the New Testament. Knowledge and love aren't at war. Love is clearly the queen, and knowledge her prince.

LOVE IS A NATIONAL TREASURE

I am going to make a confession. I'm not sure it's safe to admit this in 2020, but I like Nicolas Cage movies. There, I said it.

Honestly though, the guy won an Oscar for *Leaving Las Vegas* and then put out classics like *Con Air*, *Face/Off*, and *The Rock* all within three years! Yes, I am feeling insecure about my confession and am now defending it. Since we live in the Philadelphia area, my kids especially like the movie *National Treasure*. This list in 2 Peter reminds me of the plot of *National Treasure*.

The movie begins with Nic Cage leading a group of bumbling dude bros who think they are looking for a treasure in the Arctic. When Nic finds an artifact that turns out to be another clue, a map to the next clue, the dude bros are sorely disappointed. They mistook the map for the treasure. And what's enticing is that each clue could have fetched them thousands of dollars. If it were up to the dude bros, they probably would have stopped at the artifact, turned it in for 100 G's, and called it a day. But Nic is too smart and self-controlled for that. He knows the difference between a clue and the treasure, and he isn't stopping until he gets the treasure. Which he does. And it's worth $10 billion. Which, by the way, is estimated to be the second-highest treasure in fiction (with Smaug's riches in *The Hobbit* coming in first at a cool $62 billion).[3]

If we think of each of the words in Peter's list as clues, the connection is clear. When we think that knowing facts is the end goal, we mistake the map for the treasure. Knowledge is a tool, a very important tool, to get to the treasure. We have to find a way to let it be important but not become the treasure we are searching for.

It is ironic that we are a culture obsessed with finding the truth, being convinced it will lead to love. I have found that truth is a poor guide toward love, and my energy is better spent living with the treasure than searching frantically for the map.

WHEN WE THINK THAT KNOWING FACTS IS THE END GOAL, WE MISTAKE THE MAP FOR THE TREASURE.

As an aside, as someone who thrives and naturally lives in his head, I am here to tell you the Christian system is tilted heavily in my favor. I excelled in Sunday school and seminary and as a pastor because I was admired and respected for my smarts. The whole system is built around privileging our intellect. For most of us, we even equate belief with "thinking thoughts in our minds." I'd like to go on record to say, "That needs to change. We need to listen to people who have been marginalized for how they connect to God in ways that, frankly, may well be closer to the faith that Jesus and the New Testament espouse than to what has been set up in Christendom over the course of history."

Paul argues similarly in 1 Corinthians 13:1–13, which he often does at the end of his letters.

> If I speak in the tongues of men or of angels, but do not have love, I am only a resounding gong or a clanging cymbal. If I have the gift of prophecy and can fathom all mysteries and all knowledge, and if I have a faith that can move mountains, but do not have love, I am nothing. If I give all I possess to the poor and give over my body to hardship that I may boast, but do not have love, I gain nothing.
>
> Love is patient, love is kind. It does not envy, it does not boast, it is not proud. It does not dishonor others, it is

not self-seeking, it is not easily angered, it keeps no record of wrongs. Love does not delight in evil but rejoices with the truth. It always protects, always trusts, always hopes, always perseveres.

Love never fails. But where there are prophecies, they will cease; where there are tongues, they will be stilled; where there is knowledge, it will pass away. For we know in part and we prophesy in part, but when completeness comes, what is in part disappears. When I was a child, I talked like a child, I thought like a child, I reasoned like a child. When I became a man, I put the ways of childhood behind me. For now we see only a reflection as in a mirror; then we shall see face to face. Now I know in part; then I shall know fully, even as I am fully known.

And now these three remain: faith, hope and love. But the greatest of these is love.

His point? Everything is in service to love. Notice he includes knowledge as one of those tools. Without love, the map is just a map.

IF KNOWLEDGE IS A TOOL, WHAT ARE WE BUILDING?

Knowledge, when properly situated, can be a powerful tool toward love. And when improperly situated, it can be a powerful tool toward control and fear. If knowledge is a tool, we can use it to build up trust, freedom, and love, or we can use it to build up fear, control, and hatred.

In the same letter as his famous "Love" section, Paul presents the same scenario: true knowledge knows its place—a tool for love. False knowledge gets ahead of itself as it uses information as a way to put itself above or ahead of others. Paul writes, "Now about food sacrificed to idols: We know that 'We all possess knowledge.' But knowledge puffs up while love builds up. Those who think they know something do not yet know as they ought to know. But whoever loves God is known by God" (1 Corinthians 8:1–3). He ends this section by showing what happens if we use our knowledge for fear and control: "So this weak brother or sister, for whom Christ died, is destroyed by your knowledge" (8:11).

This is a problem with American Christianity right now. There are far too many of us who desire to be puffed up rather than to build up. And as a result, there are far too many brothers and sisters who are being destroyed by puffed-up people who pursue knowledge as a means to control rather than as a means to love.

This used to be me. So I understand. For me, the need to control wasn't because I was a bad person. It wasn't because I was greedy for power. It was because I was afraid. I was afraid of being wrong. I was afraid of feeling like I didn't have an anchor to hold on to. The more I knew, the safer I felt. Even so, that didn't excuse the times I "destroyed" someone because I was too puffed up to make room for their feelings and opinions.

What is one way to know if someone is pursuing knowledge as a means to control rather than to love? If they use Paul's words, "speaking the truth in love," as a "get out of jail free" card for using their opinions about faith as a weapon.

The most extreme example is Westboro Baptist Church in Topeka, Kansas. Church members tour the United States, picketing and protesting pretty much anything they can get their hands on. Their goal: to let people know that "God hates fags" and that all proud sinners should "repent or perish." Their strategy is all about telling the truth, no matter what. For them, telling the truth *is the loving thing to do*. On their original website, they had a "By the Numbers" section. Directly under an entry that read, "16,000,000,000: people that God killed in the flood," we saw this: 0—nanoseconds of sleep that WBC members lose over your opinions and feelings.[4]

How can someone say they love another human being while in the same breath say they do not care about your opinions and feelings? I know how—when they mask their fear of uncertainty as helping other people know the truth.

I hesitate to use WBC as an example. It may be the clearest, most absurd example, but that doesn't let us all off the hook for ways we judge others and call it love. And all we have to do to justify it to ourselves is pull our rendition of Paul's words off the shelf: "But I'm just speaking the truth in love."

Let's look at some less extreme examples we may run into on any given day:

- When someone insults you at Thanksgiving dinner because you disagreed with their political opinion, they are using "speaking the truth in love" as a weapon.
- When someone tells a couple living together, whom they barely know, that they are living in sin, they are using "speaking the truth in love" as a weapon.
- When a parent kicks their LGBTQ son or daughter out of the house, they are using "speaking the truth in love" as a weapon.

- When a friend slowly stops responding to your texts because you believe in evolution now, they are using "speaking the truth in love" as a weapon.

"Speaking the truth in love" should instead mean we've earned the right to share our opinions and values with others over time. But if we haven't demonstrated real and tangible love to someone, we cannot tell the truth, no matter what comes out of our mouths. It is an impossibility. Because truth is love. We can give our opinion, which may or may not be correct. Heck, we can even throw facts at people. But if we are not *in love* with the person in front of us and are not demonstrating love in real and practical ways, I would argue that we are not telling them the truth as the Bible presents truth.

SPEAKING THE TRUTH BY BEING IN LOVE

A friend of mine recently came to me with a problem. Since I spent many years as a pastor, many of my friends still come to me with their problems about faith, ethics, the Bible, or relationships. And I'm grateful to play that role for many of my friends. His problem is that his daughter is sleeping with her boyfriend, and he feels this is a sin. His wife has told him that if he makes too much of it, he will lose his relationship with his daughter, but he feels compelled to let his daughter know his conviction.

To summarize, he is wrestling with this tug-of-war between truth and love. He came to me with tears in his eyes and asked my opinion about what he should do. My response: "Love without judgment." I asked him why he felt the need to make sure his daughter knew what he approved of or didn't approve of in her life. She hadn't asked for his opinion. And more importantly, given the fact that she grew up in his house, I told him I was sure she already knew his opinion and what he valued. She knew his opinion about her choice, but she wasn't sure whether her dad would love and accept her unconditionally, even if she made a choice he didn't approve of. His opinion about her decision wasn't in question; his ability to love her even if she made a decision that went against his opinion was.

He sighed in relief as tears welled up. He knew this all along. He just needed someone to let him off the hook. Somehow he had come to believe it was his Christian duty to tell people his opinion about their moral decisions. He had come to believe that "speaking the truth in love" was about telling people where they are messing up. But speaking the truth in love is about demonstrating truth by your love and loving people by walking in the truth.

At root is the fear that if we don't tell people they are wrong, and if they don't feel the discomfort of our judgment, they'll have no incentive to change. But that's not how change works—not in the Bible, not in psychology, not in real life. It's amazing to me that we're still convinced that telling people they are wrong is the way to bring about real change in the world, despite it almost never working. I have seen hundreds of lives changed by human beings who have shown up to love without judgment, without feeling compelled to "speak the truth in love." I have seen almost no lives change when we begin by "speaking the truth in love."

One of my all-time favorite songs is called "Roll Away Your Stone" by the band Mumford and Sons. One stanza perfectly illustrates what I mean. It's basically a brief retelling of the lost son parable told by Jesus. The stanza's last two lines go like this: "It's not the long walk home that will change this heart, but the welcome I receive with every start."

Somehow in American Christianity, we have become convinced that it is, in fact, "the long walk home" that will change people's hearts. But it's not. It's the welcome that people receive with the love required to give someone another start.[5]

Influential psychologist Carl Rogers said it succinctly: "The curious paradox is that when I accept myself as I am, then I change."[6] This is often called the acceptance paradox or the change paradox in psychology.

When we try to "speak the truth in love," we short-circuit the process and ask people to change without first accepting themselves for who they are. We get it all backward. It's not that people don't change without judgment from others; it's that people don't change without acceptance from others. This counterintuitive truth is exactly one of the points we take from Jesus' telling of the parable of the lost son in Luke 15.

I believe the Bible tells us that the highest form of truth is wisdom, and the highest form of wisdom is love. So my highest commitment is to transformation through love and not through knowledge of facts. The great lie we've been sold in the modern era is that the only way to truth and transformation is through factfinding and making sure that people know we know our facts.

TRUTH IS AN IDOL

The Bible is straight-up weird. This is one reason it's good to have non-Christian friends who can keep us honest when we start to think that cutting off a woman's hand because she squeezes a man's testicles when her husband is losing a fight to said man is a good idea (Deuteronomy 25:11–12). If you've read your Bible over and over since you were a kid, you start to get desensitized to it all.

I always thought of idols as strange stone dolls that represented a foreign god. But if that's the only way you think of idols, you'll skip a weird point in the familiar story of the golden calf in Exodus 32.

Let's start with a little context. The Israelites were refugees in Egypt. There had been a famine in their land, and they sought asylum, which Egypt openly granted because they had been helped through their own famine by an Israelite named Joseph. Then the administration changed, and a new pharaoh took the throne. He became afraid or cautious (sometimes we can easily get those confused) about these refugees who were getting a little too numerous for the administration's comfort. He worried that if war broke out, the Israelites would side with their enemy. So he enslaved them, turning them into bricklayers and field workers, building Egypt on their backs. It's amazing how often fear leads to slavery.

In any case, the Israelites called out to God, and God heard them. Through demonstrations of power to defeat Pharaoh and the Egyptian gods, God liberated the Israelites through a man named Moses. After the Israelites wandered in the desert for a few months, God showed up in dramatic fashion on a mountain called Sinai:

> When Moses went up on the mountain, the cloud
> covered it, and the glory of the LORD settled on Mount

Sinai. For six days the cloud covered the mountain, and on the seventh day the LORD called to Moses from within the cloud. To the Israelites the glory of the LORD looked like a consuming fire on top of the mountain. Then Moses entered the cloud as he went on up the mountain. And he stayed on the mountain forty days and forty nights.

Exodus 24:15–18

This is a very ominous picture. A very powerful God showed up and liberated Israel through death and destruction. They spent two months in the desert and ended up at the foot of a mountain that "trembled violently" (Exodus 19:18) because God was sitting on top in the form of a fire so ferocious that it looked like the entire mountaintop was ablaze. Oh, yeah, and the Israelites had to stay at the foot of the mountain because if they were to come up, God would "break out against them" (19:24).

I say all this to set up what happened next. It's against this backdrop that Moses went up the mountain and wasn't seen or heard from for forty days. So when we get to Exodus 32 and the people assume God has killed Moses, it seems pretty reasonable. After all, God hadn't really come across as all that tame and stable thus far. The Bible says, "When the people saw that Moses was so long in coming down from the mountain, they gathered around Aaron and said, 'Come, make us gods who will go before us. As for this fellow Moses who brought us up out of Egypt, we don't know what has happened to him'" (32:1).

The people basically wanted God to tone it down. So Aaron concocted a plan. He asked for everyone's jewelry, and the Bible says, "He took what they handed him and made it into an idol cast in the shape of a calf, fashioning it with a tool. Then they said, 'These are your gods, Israel, who brought you up out of Egypt.' When Aaron saw this, he built an altar in front of the calf and announced, 'Tomorrow there will be a festival to the LORD'" (Exodus 32:4–5).

What we don't get in this translation is that Aaron wasn't presenting the people with *new* gods. He clearly said (in the Hebrew this is clearer), "This is your God, Israel, who brought you up out of Egypt." We know this because he got even more specific in the next verse: "he built an altar . . . and announced, 'Tomorrow there will be a festival to the LORD.'"

This calf isn't supposed to be a different God. This isn't your garden-variety idol—a stone representation of a foreign god. It's supposed to be a tamer version of Yahweh, the Lord.[7]

We often think of idols as little stone statues that primitive and ignorant ancient people worshiped as gods. But that's naive. Idols are trickier than that. In Exodus 32, Aaron called the idol "the LORD [Yahweh]," and its authority is even derived, because *this* God is the one who liberated the Israelites from Egypt. In a few strategic moves, the terrifying and unpredictable God is replaced with a God we have tamed and can control. The dangerous idols aren't *other gods* but Yahweh in disguise. The most devious and dangerous idol is the one we embrace when we replace the wild and unpredictable Yahweh with a God we can understand and a God who serves our deep need to feel safe, certain, and in control.

I believe absolute truth has become one of the church's golden calves. I know it was for me. Slowly and sneakily, I put *feeling certain* in place of God. I put *feeling grounded in absolute truth* in place of Yahweh. Beware of falling in love with cows.

It didn't help that my earliest experiences in Sunday school featured a well-intentioned teacher who got up, held up a Bible, and proclaimed it as the Word of God. Six-year-olds aren't great at knowing the difference between God and the Word of God. So the Bible became a golden calf. It was as though my Sunday school teacher was my Aaron, holding up the Bible to say, "This is your God, who brought you up out of Egypt." My middle school experience with church involved, over and over again, a well-intentioned teacher who held up the idea of absolute truth and proper belief and proclaimed, "This is Yahweh, who brought you up out of Egypt."

As a pastor, I, too, was guilty of idolatry when I held up a Bible and proclaimed, "This is the Word of God, who brings you up out of oppression and liberates your life." Ironically, the Bible itself only ever calls Jesus himself the Word of God. But it's very difficult to tame that Word. It's very difficult to turn Jesus into a set of beliefs that get consecrated as truth. But we do. Somehow when Jesus says, "I am the way and the truth and the life," we think that has something to do with the Bible. Over time, we have made the Bible itself a golden calf—not as another god, but as Jesus himself. I can remember many times in my life when Jesus and the Bible were used interchangeably. Because it gave us truth, the Bible could liberate our lives. Because it provided us with certainty, the Bible gave us peace.

We are a stiff-necked people. But understandably so. Following after love is a dangerous affair. All along the way on this journey to true love we create idols, because idols are safe. We are ever allured by the prospect of knowing for sure. In a world of constant change, constant danger, and an anxiety-producing amount of information, a golden calf feels really good.

When God is ever elusive, never showing up directly but always behind a cloud or in a clap of thunder, when we seem to be surrounded by Moseses—those who claim to have had a direct experience with God and who seem to be glowing with confidence—the golden calf of truth is seductive and promising.

But just like all idols, it cannot deliver. Literally or figuratively. It is not the Deliverer, and it will break its promise. People who claim they can give you absolute truth are channeling the serpent in Genesis, who promises a shortcut to becoming like God. There is no shortcut for being like God, because we are not God.

When we knock truth off the pedestal we've put it on and begin to realize that what we believe, or don't believe, isn't nearly as important as how we believe, we begin to realize that this great chasm we have made between truth telling and loving actions is a mistake. It's time we tore down the idol of truth and put in its place what rightfully belongs at the heart of the Christian life: love.

CHAPTER FOUR

TRUTH WITHOUT LOVE ISN'T TRUE

As we have established, beliefs are tools that can be used to control or to love. Having the *correct* belief doesn't tell us much of anything. But it's tempting because it's easy. Already in the Bible, we have people who say that what matters is what you believe. James has this to say about that:

> What good is it, my brothers and sisters, if someone claims to have faith but has no deeds? Can such faith save them? Suppose a brother or a sister is without clothes and daily food. If one of you says to them, "Go in peace; keep warm and well fed," but does nothing about their physical needs, what good is it? In the same way, faith by itself, if it is not accompanied by action, is dead.
> But someone will say, "You have faith; I have deeds."
> Show me your faith without deeds, and I will show you my faith by my deeds. You believe that there is

one God. Good! Even the demons believe that—and shudder.

James 2:14–19

I have a lot of people in my life who want me to give them a gold star because they believe in God. "Good for you," James says, "so do demons. What's your point?" Or as the rabbis would say, "He who only occupies himself with the study of the Torah is as if he had no God."[1]

Our emphasis on knowledge and belief over the past few hundred years has deceived us into thinking that *thinking true thoughts* is what matters in the Christian faith. This couldn't be further from how the Bible talks about faith and, frankly, how it talks about truth. There are almost no places in the Bible where it endorses a view of truth as "believing the right doctrine."

This reminds me of Disney's 2008 movie *Wall-E*. Earth has become a wasteland, and humans are living on a luxury spaceship called *Axiom*. The spaceship is designed so that people never have to walk. The people sit in floating chairs with giant screens in front of them and can make their way wherever they want without taking a step. Or, better yet, robots bring them whatever they want. Over time they lose their ability to walk due to obesity and lack of exercise.

Sometimes I wonder if we Christians are a little like the humans on *Axiom*. I wonder if we have become atrophied in actually practicing our faith. Sometimes I think we've convinced ourselves that we are practicing a healthy faith by simply checking off a list of four or five beliefs that make sure we are "in" and those who disagree are "out." If that's what it means to be a Christian, then we never have to walk. We can just sit in our chairs with giant screens in front of us. We have figured out a way to be a Christian without actually having to do anything to be a Christian except mentally check off a few thoughts. To that I want to say, "Good for you! You believe in God. You believe in the Bible. You believe in Jesus. So do demons. What's your point?"

Somehow we've duped ourselves into thinking that *what* we believe is more important than *how* we believe. Perhaps it's time to remember that love matters more than just believing in God in our heads and that love is a verb.[2] It's time to get off those chairs to find active ways to love the people around us.

THOUGHTS AND PRAYERS ARE NOT ENOUGH

On April 20, 1999, Columbine High School students Eric Harris and Dylan Klebold set up pipe bombs in their school cafeteria and then shot and killed twelve of their fellow students and a teacher and injured twenty-three more people. The pipe bombs fortunately never detonated. In the press conference that immediately followed, President Bill Clinton ended his remarks with, "The prayers of the American people are with you."

Since then, there have been numerous mass shootings in America, many of which have been followed by politicians offering their "thoughts and prayers." The turning point for social media acceptance came after the Umpqua Community College shooting in October 2015 that left eight students and one professor dead. An analysis of Twitter data showed that 49 percent of social media users were critical of that response, up significantly from the 23 percent figure after the June 2015 Charleston shooting. President Obama encapsulated it in a news conference in response to the shooting: "Our thoughts and prayers are not enough. It's not enough. It does not capture the heartache and grief and anger that we should feel, and it does nothing to prevent this carnage from being inflicted someplace else in America, next week or a couple months from now." By the Santa Fe shooting of 2018, 90 percent of social media users were critical of those who used "thoughts and prayers" as a response to mass shootings.[3]

In March 2019, a man attacked a mosque in Christchurch, New Zealand, killing fifty-one people and injuring forty-nine others. Within a month of its first mass shooting, New Zealand politicians came together and voted 119–1 to ban military-style semi-automatic weapons.[4]

Jesus spoke these words in Mark 12:30–31: "'Love the Lord your God with all your heart and with all your soul and with all your mind and with all your strength.' The second is this: 'Love your neighbor as yourself.' There is no commandment greater than these." Which government acted as a neighbor? Who was loving? Was it the politicians who "believed" killing people was wrong and offered their prayers? Or was it the politicians who exhibited true love through their actions?

Just as politicians have finally started to come under intense criticism for responding to mass shootings in America with *thoughts and prayers* rather than with decisive action, it is not the beliefs we hold that determine the truth of Christianity but how we live our lives. It is not our thoughts and prayers that ultimately count but our decisive action.

Now, most of us aren't politicians who can create policy to enact change. But I, too, do exactly what I criticize politicians for doing.

Social media encourages the myth that who we are is defined by the opinions we type. But the older I get, the less interested I am in how well people can script their beliefs in front of a computer and the more interested I am in how tenaciously they go about grinding out their moral existence. I'm impressed when someone can get up every single day, determined to be a better human being than he or she was yesterday. Typing out what we "stand for" is easy. But loving well isn't. I am not down on typing out our opinions—clearly. I'm only down on thinking that typing in and of itself constitutes an ethical life. May we stop thinking that becoming the kind of person we want to be is as easy as typing "me too" at those we agree with and "stupid people" at those we don't. That's a distraction from the real work of being human. And I'm ready to work.

It's no accident that I chose a political example to make this point. Besides religion, the only other area I know of where we fight so much about opinions is politics. For many of us, our faith informs our politics, so it's no surprise they would be so related. I plead with you to learn to love your political enemy. And if your impulse is to think that the greatest form of love is to convince someone to come to "your side," by whatever means necessary, I would ask you to reconsider.

The idea of "speaking the truth in love" has been taken captive by this larger culture, where how good we are as people just consists in having the right opinion about an issue and then telling as many people as possible.

We are patted on the back by our tribe when we say something negative about the "other side," and we are shunned when we say something about the common ground on which we both stand.

I'm not suggesting that learning to love our neighbor is easy. However, I am pretty sure that learning to love our enemy is harder. But I think part of the answer is to start believing that *how we believe* reveals our love just as much as, if not more than, *what we believe*.

We have privileged the *what* of our belief instead of the *how* of belief. And whether we like it or not, the content of our belief, insofar as it stays in our brains, makes zero impact on the people around us. How we enact and embody our beliefs is ultimately what matters.

When I was a pastor, I used to have lunch once a month with my friend Josh. I got to know Josh because he came to the class I mentioned earlier—For Skeptics Only. He was an atheist, but his family members were Christians, so he came to the church to support them. We came to realize we had a good connection and were good conversation partners, so we started having lunch together regularly. I learned a lot from Josh that I think can help us Christians learn to love better.

One great example is how Josh showed up to church every week. He loved with his hands and feet by sacrificing his own beliefs for his family. Now when I say "sacrifice," I don't mean that he "gave up" his beliefs and started believing in God. No, I mean he gave up his Sunday mornings each week, woke up on a day when he could have slept in, to support his wife in her belief of a God he didn't believe in. And he even hung out with her tribe each week.

How many of us have people in our lives we're close to who don't have the same political and religious beliefs we do? I have found it difficult to love people I don't know. Getting to know people who are not like us is a great step toward loving people with our hands and feet rather than just pretending we love them by having the right opinions.

Where might we all consider sacrificing our beliefs for other humans? Again, I don't mean "give up" our convictions, but I mean prioritizing love and showing up in places and spaces that make us uncomfortable, that go *against* the grain of our beliefs, to show support to those who are different from us but deserve every bit of our love because they are made in God's image.

We have a good example of this in Jesus, who spent a good deal of time with people he disagreed with at a fundamental political and moral level. For example, Mark 2:15 reads, "While Jesus was having dinner at Levi's house, many tax collectors and sinners were eating with him and his disciples, for there were many who followed him."

Do you think that Republicans are sinning by the way they cast their votes? Do you think it's a sin to be a Democrat? Perhaps it's time to invite them to dinner. And while you're eating, perhaps ask yourself what it means to love them well as you look them in the eye and see in them God's image.

THE DIFFICULTY OF BEING CHRISTIAN

In the early 1800s, there was a tall man with a humpback whose pants were too short and whose sharp wit and biting sarcasm made him equal parts intriguing and annoying to be around. He firmly believed his family was cursed because of his father and that he and all his siblings would die before age thirty-three, the age at which Jesus died. This was actually a well-founded belief—by the time he was twenty-five, five out of his six siblings had already died, as well as his mom and dad.

His death at the age of forty-two would normally have seemed to be a tragedy, but in his case, he felt like he was already on borrowed time. He began the ordination process in the Lutheran Church, the state-ordained church in his home country of Denmark, but he never was ordained. At least part of the reason was his scathing rebuke of the church that he felt had become more of a social club than anything resembling Jesus. From 1841 until his death in 1850, he published a remarkable twenty-two books, which continue to influence theologians, philosophers, and pastors today. That number is more impressive when you recognize they were all written after he received his PhD at age twenty-eight and before he was forty.

This man was Søren Kierkegaard, and he was adamant that Christianity needed to be more than thoughts and prayers and that truth was love in action. The Bible, he argued, knew nothing of this "believe in abstract doctrine" Christianity but pictured truth as more personal, more subjective, and more existential than that:

> When Christ came into the world it was difficult to become a Christian, and for this reason one did not become preoccupied with trying to understand it. Now we have almost reached the parody that to become a Christian is nothing at all, but it is a difficult and very involved task to understand it. Everything is reversed. Christianity is transformed into a kind of worldview, a way of thinking about life, and the task of faith consists in understanding and articulating it. But faith essentially

relates itself to existence, and *becoming* a Christian is what is important. Believing in Christ and wanting to "understand" his way by articulating it and elaborating on it is actually a cowardly evasion that wants to shirk the task. To become a Christian is the ultimate, to want to "understand" Christianity, as if it were some doctrine, is open to suspicion.[5]

In other words, the call of Christianity is to imitate Jesus, not to try to understand Christianity. Kierkegaard is pointing out how we have, very slowly and likely unconsciously, turned Christianity into a mental exercise. Being a "good Christian" has become about being able to understand it and articulate it. The goal, however, he will argue, is to be Christian, not to understand it. He is trying to wrest away our security blanket and show us how trying to be right actually keeps us from loving like Jesus.

I ended up hurting a number of people before I realized just how wrong I had been about Christianity. I thought the best Christians were the ones who knew the most. It turns out that the best Christians are the ones who love the most, regardless of what they know or don't know. It was a revelation to me as I looked around and found that the most simpleminded but happiest people in my congregation were the ones who loved best. They didn't get trapped in the nuances of morality or deep theological conundrums; they simply took Jesus at his word and accepted and loved everyone. It wasn't the smartest people in my congregation who showed up with items to donate for the local food drive. It wasn't the most educated who regularly invited me and my family over for dinner to make sure we felt supported. It was the people who, when I tried to talk theology, would wave their hand at me and say, "I don't understand all that. Sounds complicated."

If we're going to move forward toward a life of love, we have to begin by dismantling our dependency on "needing to know." As Kierkegaard says elsewhere, "Truth in the sense in which Christ is the truth is not a sum of statements, not a definition etc., but a life. The being of truth is not the direct redoubling of being in relation to thinking . . . No, the being of truth is the redoubling of truth within yourself, within me, within him, that your life, my life, his life is approximately the being of the truth in the striving for it, just as the truth was in Christ a *life*, for he was the truth. And therefore, Christianly understood, truth is obviously not to know the truth but to be the truth."[6]

Or again, he summarizes: "What I am referring to . . . is very plain and simple, namely, that truth for the particular individual is truth only insofar as the individual itself produces it in action."[7]

Since 2017, I have cohosted a podcast with Bible scholar Pete Enns called *The Bible for Normal People*. Since starting the podcast, we've had incredible conversations with artists, pastors, scholars, influential leaders, and normal people about Christian belief and what the Bible teaches.

As a result, people regularly ask me what I believe about God and the Bible. My response is as genuine as I can muster: I don't know. That's right. I don't know what I believe about all the doctrine surrounding the Bible and God. You'll probably get a more accurate answer if you ask the people who know me best. I learned long ago that I'm far too self-deceptive to answer that question honestly.

For example, do I believe in Jesus' resurrection? We most often ask that expecting that we answer based on an idea we have in our head. As though that's what's important. The better question is this: Do we trust in Jesus' resurrection? To be honest, that's a question that can only be answered by watching someone's behavior. Otherwise, instead of the resurrection being something that transforms lives and changes how we treat one another, it becomes a fact that we simply check off the list in our head. To "believe" in the resurrection is not a matter of saying, "Yes, I believe that," but to live a resurrection life that pursues resurrection in our everyday life.

- Every time I see someone and feel like I'm better than they are, I show that I do not trust in Jesus' resurrection.
- Every time I'm uncomfortable sitting next to a transgender person on a plane, I show that I do not trust in Jesus' resurrection.
- Every time I insist on my way without considering the needs of my spouse, I show that I do not trust in Jesus' resurrection.

What does it matter to the world and to the people around me if I check off "belief in Jesus' resurrection" as a fact but it doesn't inform how I live my life? When someone asks me, "What do you believe?" I'm more likely to answer what I wish I believed than what I actually believe. If you're just going by what's in your head, what's the difference between what you actually believe and what you wish you believed? Almost none.

TRUTH IS LOVE IN ACTION

It is the Bible itself that calls us back to this understanding of truth. John (in his gospel, as well as in his letters—1, 2, and 3 John) uses the word *truth* more than any other writer in the Bible. Not one time does he use it to refer to "accurate beliefs." But over and over again, he uses it to encourage Christians to "walk in the truth."

In 1 John 1:6, John writes, "If we claim to have fellowship with him [Jesus] and yet walk in the darkness, we lie and do not live out the truth." Did you catch that? We lie and do not do what is true. I thought we were just supposed to *believe what is true*. Well, John didn't get the memo. Or again, John writes, "Dear children, let us not love with words or speech but with actions and in truth" (1 John 3:18).

One of his favorite metaphors is the idea that we don't *believe* the truth; we *walk* in it. He writes, "It has given me great joy to find some of your children walking in the truth, just as the Father commanded us" (2 John 4). And again, "I have no greater joy than to hear that my children are walking in the truth" (3 John 4). In other words, truth isn't a thought we have in our heads but an action we live out in our everyday, walking-around lives.

It surprised me a bit to find that, of all the instances of the word *truth* in the Bible, both in the Old and New Testaments, only in the letters to Timothy and to the Thessalonians does anything like "it's important to defend accurate ideas about Jesus" come up.[8] And not surprisingly, since the Bible wasn't finished while it was being written, there are zero references to the importance of defending accurate ideas about the Bible.[9]

How does the Bible think of truth? It is not abstract belief but a concrete set of behaviors toward other people and God. It's love in action. Let's look at a few examples.

The most common way the Bible uses the word *truth* is to talk about *faithfulness* and *trustworthiness*, which, if you think about it, are two sides of the same coin.

Here is the first use of the word most commonly translated as "truth" in the Bible: "Then the man bowed down and worshiped the LORD, saying, "Praise be to the LORD, the God of my master Abraham, who has not abandoned his kindness and *faithfulness* to my master. As for me, the LORD has led me on the journey to the house of my master's relatives" (Genesis 24:26–27, italics added).

Notice that the word *truth* isn't here. It's not even translated "truth" in the NIV translation; it's translated "faithfulness." That should give us a clue as to what the word means most often in context.[10] Truth is a character trait, not an abstract idea. The reason we tell the truth as we see it is not to make sure people get an accurate picture of the real world, but so we can be counted on not to deceive others but to be faithful people. The real desire, especially in the Old Testament, isn't for people to be right about how the world works in all of its historical and scientific intricacies, but for people to live rightly—*faithfully*—with other people, not to be liars and deceivers.

You can see the same sharp contrast anytime someone says, "Well, technically, I didn't lie." If you ever hear that, you know that someone is trying to cover over their deception with the "truth." The Bible, however, isn't interested so much in "technicalities" as in the character and heart of the person speaking.

The New Testament also uses as its primary definition of

truth the idea of faithfulness. We see this in the first use of *truth* in the New Testament: "Teacher," they said, "we know that you are a man of integrity and that you teach the way of God in accordance with the truth. You aren't swayed by others, because you pay no attention to who they are" (Matthew 22:16). In other words, truth is about integrity and not adjusting what you say to please others. This is made clear in Luke 20:21: "Teacher, we know that you speak and teach what is right, and that you do not show partiality but teach the way of God in accordance with the truth."

If we consider "faithfulness" the root meaning of truth in the Bible, then being honest, being fair and accurate in your judgments, and behaving in ethical ways are its branches.

Back to 1 John 1:6. We see again that *honesty*, or *telling the truth*, is one of the ways *truth* is used in the Bible: "If we claim to have fellowship with him and yet walk in the darkness, we lie and do not live out the truth."[11] This reinforces the idea that truth is not a belief but an action. John tells us that we need to "live out the truth," not just believe in it.

We see *fair and accurate testimony* as one of the meanings of *truth* in the Bible. In John 5:31–35, we find these words of Jesus:

> "If I testify about myself, my testimony is not true. There is another who testifies in my favor, and I know that his testimony about me is true.
>
> "You have sent to John and he has testified to the truth. Not that I accept human testimony; but I mention it that you may be saved. John was a lamp that burned and gave light, and you chose for a time to enjoy his light."[12]

Interestingly, in this same section, Jesus points out that the Scriptures can be a stumbling block to finding Jesus. He says in 5:39–40: "You study the Scriptures diligently because you think that in them you have eternal life. These are the very Scriptures that testify about me, yet you refuse to come to me to have life."

In other words, when we fixate on a life of getting the right beliefs and think the Bible is the only place to get those beliefs, we can miss out on seeing the Jesus who is right in front of us. Some may say, "But Jesus has long since died, and the only way to get to know Jesus is through the Bible." To that I would say, "Jesus is dead?" What does it mean to "believe in the resurrection of Jesus" if you believe that the only way to experience Jesus today is through a book?

Lastly, we see that *truth* means *ethical behavior* in a few passages. For example, Proverbs 8:7 reads, "My mouth speaks what is true, for my lips detest wickedness." And in Isaiah 38:3, we read, "Remember, LORD, how I have walked before you faithfully and with wholehearted devotion and have done what is good in your eyes."

In other words, truth isn't the opposite of falsehood, as we might assume today, but the opposite of wickedness. In fact, in the Isaiah 38 example, it's all tied back to faithfulness. Being faithful to God is about doing "what is good in God's eyes." The word behind "faithfulness" in that verse? You guessed it—it's what is elsewhere translated "truth."

John picks up on this in his famous passage in John 3:19–21, where Jesus is talking to Nicodemus. After he delivers his famous "For God so loved the world" line, Jesus says this: "This is the verdict: Light has come into the world, but people loved darkness instead of light because their deeds were evil. Everyone who does evil hates the light, and will not come into the light for fear that their deeds will be exposed. But whoever lives by the truth comes into the light, so that it may be seen plainly that what they have done has been done in the sight of God."

We must *live* by the truth, by which Jesus clearly means living a life of goodness and not evil. If we live by the truth, we fear nothing because we have nothing to hide. This touches on another use of the word *truth* in the New Testament: truth as *authenticity*. But this idea is important enough to warrant its own chapter, coming soon.

FROM "TRUTH IN LOVE" TO TRUE LOVE

So what does the Bible ask of us when it comes to truth? It almost never asks us to "believe in it," and it almost never asks us to "get it right." In fact, we have example after example of people in the Bible getting God and Jesus wrong. It's clear throughout the Gospels that the disciples do not understand what Jesus is up to.

The Bible asks us to walk in truth, which is defined as:

- faithfulness
- trustworthiness
- honesty and fair testimony
- authenticity
- commitment to doing good

Let's go back to bell hooks's definition of love from chapter 2: "the will to extend one's self for the purpose of nurturing one's own or another's spiritual growth" through using these ingredients: "care, affection, recognition, respect, commitment, and trust, as well as honest and open communication."[13] If we map these uses of truth in the Bible onto the love ingredients bell hooks gives us, we see profound and significant overlap:

- commitment *as* faithfulness
- trust *as* trustworthiness
- honesty *as* honesty and fair testimony
- openness *as* authenticity
- care, affection, and recognition *as* commitment to doing good

That's right. There is no tension between truth and love in the Bible, because if we look closely at how the Bible *actually* talks about love, there is significant overlap, almost to the point that they cannot be separated.

If you grew up as a Christian in the 1990s, you would have been part of a gloriously weird subculture. There were traveling strongmen who could rip telephone books in half and break blocks of ice and baseball bats, all for Jesus. In fact, I was baptized by that group of former wrestlers and football players. There were TV shows like *McGee and Me!* and radio shows like *Adventures in Odyssey.* Then there was the music—Audio Adrenaline, Newsboys, and the pinnacle of Christian music in the 1990s, DC Talk. One of their hit songs was called "Luv Is a Verb" and had such poetic lines as, "And yo that's when it hit me, that luv is a verb."

The point of the song, of course, is that love is more than words we say to each other. As the apostle John writes, "Dear children, let us not love with words or speech but with actions and in truth" (1 John 3:18). DC Talk was singing to remind Christians that we shouldn't make light of love. We said we loved McDonald's, the new Walkman, and Zack Morris. We loved ice cream, walks in the park and working out, and our latest Reebok Pump shoes. Love became something we *said*, not something we *did*. The Bible, however, reminds us that true love doesn't happen with words only, but with actions as well.

It hit me a few years ago that the same can be said for "truth." We think that truth is a noun. It's a thing. Out there. But what we see in these verses in John is that for the Bible, truth isn't in our head but in our hands and feet. There isn't much conversation in the Bible around whether a story is true. But we have plenty of real estate taken up by the question, "Do we walk truthfully?"

In the Bible, truth is an *ethical* category, not an intellectual one. It's a *relational* category, not an individual one. We see this with Paul's statement in Ephesians 4:15 about "speaking the truth in love."

This tension we have felt between truth and love disappears when we consider how truth is defined throughout the Bible. There is no tension, because truth is an action—and the highest action we can take to walk in the truth is to love others. John says it best in 2 John 4–6:

> It has given me great joy to find some of your children walking in the truth, just as the Father commanded us. And now, dear lady, I am not writing you a new command but one we have had from the beginning. I ask that we love one another. And this is love: that we walk in obedience

to his commands. As you have heard from the beginning, his command is that you walk in love.

Let's take a minute to ponder this argument John is making:

- The Father has commanded us to walk in the truth.
- This commandment isn't new but the one we've always had: love one another.
- What is love? That we walk in obedience to his commands.
- What is his command? That we walk in love.

Confused yet? John seems to be going in circles here. I would argue he's not going in circles because he ends somewhere different than he starts. He begins by saying God's command is that we walk in truth. He ends by saying God's command is that we walk in love. These, he says, are not different commands but the same love.

To walk in love *is* to walk in truth. And these are both *actions*.

LOVE IS EMBODIED TRUTH

Love is embodied truth, or as we will call it for the rest of this book—true love. The Bible doesn't spend much time focusing on fact-truths or even meaning-truths. The Bible does point us to the importance of true love and uses facts and meaning to point us to that reality. The answer to our tension between truth and love is to see that these aren't two separate goals that we are hopelessly waffling between, but one goal and one tool to help us get there.

Perhaps truth is found not in a book but in our lives. Perhaps reading the Bible for truth is like reading the IKEA manual in hopes that the facts will be enough to magically assemble the bookshelf. Perhaps the question we should be asking isn't, "Am I getting the Bible right?" but "What kind of life is our reading of the Bible producing?"

THE QUESTION WE SHOULD BE ASKING ISN'T, "AM I GETTING THE BIBLE RIGHT?" BUT "WHAT KIND OF LIFE IS OUR READING OF THE BIBLE PRODUCING?"

Against this backdrop, I begin to feel sheepish at best, arrogant at worst, to even ask the question: *Is the Bible true?* Because the Bible never answers that question. That's why it always felt awkward when I read books that try to "prove that the Bible is true." The Bible doesn't seem to care about that question. When we ask that question of the Bible, it ignores us and answers with a better question: *Is your life true?* When I try to put the Bible under the microscope, it quickly moves to the side and pins *me* under a microscope. When I try to understand it, it simply asks if *I* am standing under it.

Notice how Jesus responds to questions that are asked of him in the Gospels. When the Pharisee asks, "Who is my neighbor?" Jesus doesn't answer with facts but tells a story that asks a better question: "Does your life reflect neighborly love?" (see Luke 10:25–37). When the rich ruler asks Jesus, "What must I do to inherit eternal life?" Jesus doesn't answer with facts or beliefs but with a command: "Sell everything you have and give to the poor" (see Luke 18:18–30).

And so when we ask, "Is the Bible true?" the Bible resists an answer. Instead it asks, "Are you living truthfully?" And if we do not know, we may ask, "Are we setting people free, including ourselves?" If not, then perhaps our beliefs aren't as close to the truth as we might think.

Truth is alluring because it promises a destination, a place of rest. But Jesus says *he* will give us rest (see Matthew 11:28). When we are weary and burdened, we go to Jesus, not to the safety we find in being right about our opinions—a way of finding rest that is unstable. And we know it's unstable, so we fight desperately to keep it. We fight against other people who disagree with us because we are so afraid of losing that feeling of safety and security.

But when we find our rest in Jesus, who is bigger than our beliefs or thoughts, we are free to explore beliefs. We are free to truly listen to other people and to allow other people to be free. Perhaps this is what Jesus means when he says that he is "the way and the truth and the life" (John 14:6). Jesus embodies true love, and if we want to find the way and the truth and the life, we must follow his example, not just think factually accurate thoughts.

When we have our faith in Jesus, it allows us to be like the man who said to Jesus, "I believe; help my unbelief!" (Mark 9:24 ESV). We have often taken this to mean, "Help me with my unbelief"—as though the goal is to move from unbelief to belief. But what if the emphasis is the help we receive, regardless of whether we are in a state of belief or unbelief? If the word *belief* in the Bible has to do with trust, then it is a relational word, not an abstract word about beliefs in our brain. And we can read "help my unbelief" in a whole new light.

CHAPTER FIVE

IF IT DOESN'T SET YOU FREE, IT'S NOT TRUE

We spent hours and hours agonizing over the names of our children. Some might have called Sarah and me "intentional," and others might have called us "thoughtful." Still others might have called us "neurotic" and "intense." If I'm being honest, they're all right.

It turns out, though, that being so intense-ional led to the names of our children mapping our spiritual journey with spectacular accuracy. Our oldest, Augustine, was named after Saint Augustine, a famous (infamous?) church father who revolutionized theology for hundreds of years. Our Augustine came at a time when I was a Calvinist, or Reformed, minister who had just graduated from seminary. While I had a lot of questions, I was pretty sure I also had a lot of answers.

Seventeen months later, we had Tov, whose name comes from the statement God makes again and again in the creation narrative. When God creates, God calls it "good" or, in Hebrew, *tov*. This represented a monumental shift for Sarah and me in our theology. Whereas Saint Augustine saw the world and humans as fundamentally sinful and bad, we began to see that God calls creation good. *Perhaps*, we thought, *humans aren't totally depraved, to use my proper Calvinist language, but tend to want to do what's right*—even if we don't always know what that means or how to do it.

With that shift, we began to see that so much of the Christianity we had experienced was about creating rules out of fear that our deeply sinful nature would get out of control. The only way to the good life was to create rules and then hope that our guilt function was deep enough to police our behavior and keep us in line.

It had become for us a religion of fear. And when there is fear, there is control. But when we went back to our Bible, it said that "perfect love drives out fear" (1 John 4:18) and that "where the Spirit of the Lord is, there is freedom" (2 Corinthians 3:17). We weren't experiencing freedom, but a fear of freedom that was masked as the noble pursuit of truth.

Seventeen months after Tov came our only daughter, Elletheia. Her name is a combination of two Greek words found in John 8:32, where Jesus says, "Then you will know the truth, and the truth will set you free." When you combine truth (*aletheia*) and freedom (*eleutheria*), you get Elletheia.

This pursuit of a truth *that sets us free* led us to freedom. But as many on this journey know, freedom can feel at first a lot like loneliness. In the moment, breaking free from a religion of rules and "fear masked as truth telling" feels uplifting. But like the Israelites who grumbled once they left Egypt, we can quickly feel like God led us out to the desert to be alone, longing for the water and food of community and connection.

Sure, we told ourselves, our old way of being Christian was suffocating us and sucking the joy out of our lives, but at least we had a lot of other people suffocating with us! Or as the Israelites said, "It would have been better for us to serve the Egyptians than to die in the desert!" (Exodus 14:12).

Once we got our bearings in the desert, however, we realized how amazing it is. We realized that God provided nourishment for us each day, and, as it turns out, the more time we spent in the desert, the more people we found who were in the same place we were. What we thought was desolate and deserted, forsaken by God, is actually a theological Burning Man, where creativity is encouraged and the pursuit of true love trumps the pursuit of truth-telling fear.

And we realized that's where true life is found—between the rules of slavery and the rules of the establishment, between Egypt and Jerusalem. For us, the spiritual life is about finding life in the freedom of the desert, not running from what was behind us but also not running into the arms of another promise of certainty and security. We found the God of Exodus, the One who is not tame, who doesn't provide purpose but presence, who doesn't promise abundance but enough—and for us, that God was where we found freedom.

And so, our happy little accident, child number four, is named Exodus.

But let's go back to our daughter, Elletheia. The more I have pondered John 8:32, the more revolutionary it has become to me. *"Then you will know the truth, and the truth will set you free."*

Growing up, I was always taught that this meant, "If you

believe the right things, you will find freedom." Sadly, for me at least, the more I tried to believe the right things, the less freedom I found. I felt trapped, constrained, controlled by the preachers and teachers who seemed to have the market cornered on "right beliefs."

But what if we put this verse under the microscope and examine it closely? Instead of thinking of it as "If you believe this set of facts, this will happen to you," what if it is giving us a *criterion* for how to tell if something is true?

To put it simply, what if we interpret this verse as saying, "If it doesn't set you free, it isn't the truth"? Truth is not a dead set of facts. It is active. It is an agent. It is in motion. It is the thing that sets us free. And so, following Paul's instruction in 1 Thessalonians 5:21 (ESV), we must "test everything; hold fast what is good." And what is the test to tell us if something is true? If it is good? Well, according to Jesus in John 8:32, the test is this: *Does it set you free?* If not, it is not true.

TRUTH IS NOT A DEAD SET OF FACTS. IT IS ACTIVE. IT IS AN AGENT. IT IS IN MOTION. IT IS THE THING THAT SETS US FREE.

We tend to privilege truth and focus on it as the way to freedom. But unfortunately we lose our way, and truth becomes the way to slavery and control. We must recognize that this path has betrayed us. We thought that getting the facts right would set us free, but instead we started policing the facts, and our church communities started thinking that love is about criticizing people for what they do and don't do. If we privilege facts, we often do not find our way to love. But if we privilege freedom and focus on it as the way to truth, we may find our way to both.

This is an incredibly important reversal. Rather than saying, "What I'm telling you is true, so you'd better find it freeing," John 8:32 can just as easily be flipped to say, "Test what I am telling you to see if it is true—you will know if it frees you."

Paul gives this idea a resounding "amen" in 2 Corinthians 3:17 when he says, "Where the Spirit of the Lord is, there is freedom." Not only is it not true if there is no freedom—it is also not of God, and the Spirit of God is not there.

This fits well with another wonderful story we have of Jesus, who in his very first sermon reads from the scroll of Isaiah:

> "The Spirit of the Lord is on me,
>   because he has anointed me
>   to proclaim good news to the poor.
> He has sent me to proclaim freedom for the prisoners
>   and recovery of sight for the blind,
> to set the oppressed free,
>   to proclaim the year of the Lord's favor."

> Then he rolled up the scroll, gave it back to the attendant and sat down. The eyes of everyone in the synagogue were fastened on him. He began by saying to them, "Today this scripture is fulfilled in your hearing."
>
> *Luke 4:18–21*

The Spirit of the Lord is on Jesus. And as Paul has told us, we know what that means: freedom isn't far behind. The Spirit of God brings freedom. In Luke, this freedom is concrete—freedom for prisoners and the oppressed. In John, this freedom is abstract—freedom from being a slave to sin. Both are correct, and both are profound.

Perhaps this is part of what Jesus means in John 14:6, since he says that he is "the way and the truth and the life." He is an active agent for freedom. And perhaps those aren't three separate things. What if "the way and the truth and the life" are three ways to say the same thing?

He's not talking about facts. He's talking about something deeper.

For some reason we have unhitched truth from freedom, and out of our fear that people will just "run amok with sin," we have understated the central value that freedom plays in the life of faith. And this freedom is not abstract. It is concrete. It isn't a thought or a belief, but a deeply personal and actual reality. We do not "believe in freedom"; we live freely and act in ways that free others.

What does it mean for a person to be the truth? It means, *I have come to set the prisoners free—and when I do, that is truth.*

TRUE LOVE LIBERATES

The wonderful poet and humanitarian Maya Angelou tells a story about her mom when she moved out of the house after getting pregnant at seventeen:

Love liberates. It doesn't just hold—that's ego. Love liberates.

When my son was born, I was seventeen. My mother had a huge house—fourteen-room house. At seventeen, I went to her and said, "I'm leaving." She asked me, "You're leaving my house?" And she had live-in help. I said, "Yes, I've found a job and I've got a room with cooking privileges down the hall, and the landlady will be the babysitter."

She asked me, "You're leaving my house?"

I said, "Yes, ma'am."

"And you're taking the baby?"

I said, "Yes."

She said, "Alright. Remember this. When you step over my doorsill, you've been raised. You know the difference between right and wrong. Do right . . . And remember this, you can always come home."

I went home every time life slammed me down and made me call it uncle. I went home with my baby. My mother never once acted as if, "I told you so." She'd say, "Oh! Baby's home! Oh my darlin'. Mama's gonna cook you something. Mother's gonna make this for you." Love! She liberated me to life. She continued to do that . . .

She released me. She freed me to say I may have something in me that would be of value—maybe not just to me. That's love.[1]

If you think about it, that's the story of God. "When you go out into the world, you've been raised. You know the difference between right and wrong. Do right. And remember this, you can always come home."

That statement encapsulates for me the liberating nature of love. It creates space for freedom and does not resent that freedom. It allows people to make choices without getting our feelings hurt that people didn't make the choice our opinion pointed them to.

True love doesn't say, "I told you so," but says, "You always have a place here." True love doesn't say, "Let me tell you my opinion of your choices for the tenth time," but says, "You know the difference between right and wrong—I don't control you, and I trust you."

That last line of Maya Angelou's interview is also incredibly important: "She freed me to say I may have something in me that would be of value—maybe not just to me."

Are we treating people in our lives in such a way that *they themselves* are coming to believe they have something of value to offer the world? *That* is the truth. How do we know it's true? Because it liberates. The truth is that which sets us free. So if it is not liberating, it is not true—no matter how accurate it is, no matter how many times you say, "I'm just sayin'," or "I'm just tellin' you the truth." If what you say is not said in a way that the other person comes away feeling more whole and more valued, it is not true.

Learning to live this liberating love is more difficult than you think. It takes wisdom to find the balance in relationships—between acceptance and enablement, between belonging and constructive criticism, between realism and hope. This is the struggle of leaving behind fact-truth and moving toward wisdom-truth.

I am forever grateful that my parents represented this balance of liberating love. They moved so beautifully between criticism, because they wanted me to have an accurate view of myself, and belief, because they wanted me to know I have value and can overcome my faults. For example, after every basketball game, they would tell me all the ways in which I messed up and all the ways in which I excelled, but always with a hug and a smile that told me I was loved and accepted, regardless of either my failures or my successes.

My parents were good at accepting me and yet were always pushing me. They let me know I would be loved, regardless of my grades, but that they would be disappointed if I didn't make straight A's because they knew I had the potential to do so. They showed worry and concern about some of my choices but always respected my autonomy. They told me I would be responsible for the consequences of my actions.

They never held back their thoughts, giving me their opinions about who I was spending time with, who I was dating, and what I spent my days doing. They were at times what we might call "brutally honest," but they never disrespected me. They prefaced things during my teen years with, "Well, it's your life, but if it were me . . ." That one phrase became so valuable to me. It provided me with advice but not control, autonomy but not apathy. Their respect came from their intuitive and implicit understanding that they, too, were flawed human beings, that their opinion was not the word of God or the absolute truth, but was their experience they wanted to share with another human being they loved deeply.

This liberating love is not easy.

LIBERATING LOVE IS LETTING PEOPLE GROW UP: BETWEEN LOVE AND CONTROL

The Buddhist monk Thich Nhat Hanh says, "You must love in such a way that the person you love feels free, not only outside but also inside."[2] So, is freedom a feeling? Freedom is much more than a feeling—but it is not less.

The tricky part about humans and freedom is the narrow line between love and control. I would say that we rarely find a person who will admit they would rather control than love. The problem is that we humans aren't always great at knowing the difference. We want to use what we know to help others. But without us really knowing when we switch from one to the other, that knowledge can liberate or it can control. And I think we all agree true love does not control. Or as our old friend Søren Kierkegaard says, "Only the unloving person fancies that he should build up by controlling the other."[3]

One of the most explicit illustrations of "control masked as love" I've come across is in the movie *Tangled*, Disney's retelling of the fairy tale "Rapunzel."[4] Gothel, Rapunzel's mother, convinces her that it's for her own good that she not be allowed out of the tower. While it's true that Rapunzel is safe in the tower, love isn't just about safety. It's also about freedom. But since Gothel's eternal life comes from Rapunzel's hair, it's clear that the real motive is control, so freedom is out of the question. This comes to a head in the song "Mother Knows Best," with lines like, "All I have is one request, Rapunzel . . . Don't ever ask to leave this tower again . . . I love you very much, dear."[5]

Whether or not someone's love is freedom affirming or controlling is found at the intersection of the *intention* and the *impact* of that love. If one's intention is good but the impact is not, something is broken, and we cannot call what has happened good. Even if you "know" what's best for someone else, often the most loving thing to do isn't to try to control their life, but to help them avoid harm. Oftentimes the control is more harming than the consequences of their action. Sometimes forcing what's best is the worst.

And to make things more complicated, is there really a difference between someone *feeling controlled* and someone *actually being controlled*? If we consider the intention and impact of a controlling love, that difference becomes almost invisible. This is why the liberating nature of love means feelings must be taken into account, as Thich Nhat Hahn has wisely recognized.

One time, my in-laws were babysitting our then three-year-old son Tov while we were out running errands. They live in a gated community. When we returned, we saw him standing at the gate with his pacifier and pillowcase—the two things he never left home without. What wasn't with him was either of his grandparents. We found my in-laws at home, frantically trying to find their grandson so they didn't have to explain to their daughter that they lost a kid. It turns out he had woken up from his nap and just walked out the door and up the sidewalk to the gate. He didn't tell anyone. Knowing his personality now, he probably didn't feel it was anyone's business to know what he was doing.

In this instance, less freedom was good for Tov. Stopping a three-year-old from wandering around a gated community is loving and freedom affirming in appropriate ways. Now that he's ten, I don't think it's so clear. Maybe it's loving and freedom affirming. Maybe it isn't. But stopping a twenty-year-old from wandering around a gated community isn't loving; it's controlling.

In other words, one way to measure between protection and control is whether or not we respect the autonomy of the person and allow them to be responsible for their choices when it makes sense for them to do so.

Things change. We change. I wonder if most of us learn how to love children and think it translates. I wonder if most of us need to learn how to love adults. Treating adults like children is one of the primary ways we end up controlling instead of showing true love—a truth and love that liberates. Instead, let us respect one another as adults who are all responsible for our own choices and then love each other, even if others make decisions about their own lives that we wouldn't make for ourselves. True love isn't a free-for-all. It's more complicated than that. It involves deep listening, deep understanding, and an acceptance that things change.

CHAPTER SIX

THE IMPORTANCE OF WEAVING FLAX INTO TABLECLOTHS

When I was in middle school, one of my favorite days of the month was the arrival of the Eastbay catalog in the mailbox. For those of you who are under thirty, a catalog is like a paper-based Amazon. It's how we used to buy things before the internet. Eastbay was a sneaker company, and I was what would nowadays be called a "sneakerhead." At its peak in high school, I had forty-three pairs. And by "it," I mean the neurosis I had that compelled me to keep buying shoes.

One day, I was in my parents' closet looking for something and noticed my dad had only three pair of shoes—work boots, weekend boots (remember, I'm from Texas), and one pair of sneakers that were probably a decade old. I asked him why he didn't have more shoes, assuming everyone would want dozens of shoes cluttering their room. I'll never forget what he told me: "I don't need new things as long as you and your sister get what you want." This was representative of all sorts of interactions with my dad—him forgoing stuff and finding joy in my sister and me partaking.

I distinctly remember walking away feeling baffled. I didn't understand what he meant. Why? It wasn't because I wasn't smart enough. It wasn't because I didn't have the facts. It was because I didn't have his perspective. I didn't get it because I hadn't experienced the love that parents have for their children. Last night, my wife was worried about my happiness, as she often is. She ended with, "I just want to make sure you're happy." My response was the same as it is every time we have this conversation: "As long as I'm doing the work I love and my family is happy, I'm happy." Once I had kids of my own and experienced what my dad experienced, the meaning of his words from twenty years before changed. I only have five pair of shoes in my closet right now and have never been happier.

You see, the *fact* that my dad only owned three pairs of shoes didn't *mean* anything to me. It had very little significance. But my life experiences have changed the meaning of that historical story. They have probably even shaped how I've told the story. Details have fallen away. Whatever else we were talking about has been forgotten, and even the exact words he used have probably been distorted. But the meaning has never been more profound. The same is true with the Bible.

TURNING WHEAT INTO BREAD

In a collection called *Seder Eliyahu Zuta*, the rabbis tell a parable about "a mortal king who had two servants whom he loved with perfect love":

To one he gave a measure of wheat and to the other he gave a measure of wheat; to one [the first, he gave] a bundle of flax and to the other a bundle of flax.

What did the clever one of the two do? He took the flax and wove it into a napkin. He took the wheat and made it into fine flour by sifting the grain first and grinding it. Then he kneaded the dough and baked it, set the loaf on the table, spread the napkin over the loaf, and left it to await the coming of the king.

But the foolish one of the two did not do anything at all.

After a while the king came into his house and said to the two servants, "My sons, bring me what I gave you." One brought out the table with the loaf baked of fine flour on it, and with the napkin spread over the bread. And the other brought out his wheat in a basket with a bundle of flax over the wheat grains. "What a shame! What a disgrace!"

What does this parable mean? The rabbis tell us: "So, too, when the Holy One gave the Torah to Israel, He gave it as wheat to be turned into fine flour and as flax to be turned into cloth for garments."[1]

In other words, God is disappointed with God's people when their fear keeps them from reinterpreting the Bible to make something new and relevant. Or as Karin Hedner Zetterholm summarizes in her book *Jewish Interpretation and the Bible*:

In other words, the parable [of the wheat and the flax] suggests that new interpretations of the biblical text are not only legitimate but desirable and even superior to the original product. According to this view, God expects humans to search for new meanings, develop and adapt the Bible to new circumstances. It is the one who engages in such a project who acts in accordance with God's will, not the one who safeguards the original meaning. The aim is not to establish the original or literal meaning of a given biblical passage, or attempt to reconstruct the circumstances in which it was composed, but rather to interpret and adapt it for contemporary times.[2]

Okay, but we're not Jewish. We're Christian. So we always have to ask that all-important question that I wore on my wrist for most of middle school: What would Jesus do?

Glad you asked, because we have an almost identical parable in our Bible, in the gospel of Matthew, where Jesus is talking about the kingdom of heaven. A master gives his servants bags of gold and then goes on a trip. Two of them invested the gold and increased the master's money. The last servant was afraid of losing the master's money, so he buried his gold in the ground to make sure he gave back what was given to him.

These are the words Jesus puts in the master's mouth:

> His master replied, "You wicked, lazy servant! So you knew that I harvest where I have not sown and gather where I have not scattered seed? Well then, you should have put my money on deposit with the bankers, so that when I returned I would have received it back with interest.
>
> "So take the bag of gold from him and give it to the one who has ten bags. For whoever has will be given more,

and they will have an abundance. Whoever does not have, even what they have will be taken from them. And throw that worthless servant outside, into the darkness, where there will be weeping and gnashing of teeth."

Matthew 25:26–30

Geez, Jesus. In the Jewish version, God just gives them a little verbal lashing and moves on. In the Christian version, the verbal lashing comes with getting kicked to the curb with a guarantee of weeping and gnashing of teeth. That's harsh, man.

We can't underestimate the power of this story when it comes to how we read our Bible. Most of us have been told to be afraid of changing the meaning of the Bible to fit our experiences of God. But these parables tell us that the real danger is not taking enough risks with the Bible, hoping that when Jesus comes back, we'll get congratulated for just burying it in the ground and not turning it into something new, different, more.

What if we moved from being passionate about discovering the "true meaning" of the Bible from two thousand years ago to being passionate about creating a "faithful meaning" of the Bible that propels us into a life of love today?

READING THE BIBLE IS LIKE BEING A CHEF

This way of thinking of the Bible reminds me of the cooking show *Top Chef*. To be honest, I don't watch too many cooking shows since I'm too busy watching documentaries and *Arrested Development* reruns. *Top Chef* is a cooking competition where chefs are given the same ingredients and asked to make a dish in a certain amount of time and sometimes with a certain theme. This show is currently in its sixteenth season and doesn't seem to be slowing down.

What I love about it is how diverse and creative the end results can be, even when contestants are given the same starting point and the same limitations. They each produce dishes that are different in taste, texture, and look.

This is exactly how we need to start thinking of truth and the Bible. Think about it. They use the same ingredients (facts) to make something unique to them, their passions, and their skills (meaning) that other people experience as good (wisdom). In the context of the two parables above, the judges wouldn't be very happy if a contestant just left the ingredients as they were given them and presented them back.

> JUDGE: "Um, you didn't do anything. You just left the ingredients in the bowl and stared at them for twenty minutes."
>
> CONTESTANT: "No, I studied them and made sure I understood why they were there in the first place. And I didn't want to disrespect the producers and assistants who put them there. I was being thoughtful. Are you saying being thoughtful is bad? I thought it was most important to conserve them just the way they were."
>
> JUDGE: "But this is a cooking show. The point is to create something new from what you are given."
>
> CONTESTANT: "Yeah, but what if I created something terrible? I would be really embarrassed—maybe I wouldn't ever be able to work as a chef again! Or what if I burned down the kitchen and hurt all these innocent people?"

JUDGE: "That's kind of the point. There's always the risk you're going to make something terrible or do something wrong to hurt someone. That's why it's important to learn how to make things that aren't terrible and use the tools in a way that makes you confident you won't hurt anyone. By the way, who's going to hire someone to cook who either never tries to create something new or just creates the same thing over and over again?"

Well, you get the picture.

Does that mean that just because we need to change the meaning of the Bible, we can make it mean whatever we want? No. That's our perfectionism talking again. We have to stop thinking in either/or. There's a very important place between "there's only one thing the Bible can mean" and "the Bible can mean anything we want it to."[3]

Just like in the cooking show: the raw materials are there, but they can be put together in dozens, if not hundreds, of different ways. Some of those make more sense than others. Some taste better than others. Some are flat-out bad. It's a spectrum of better or worse interpretations.

What if we changed our perspective from thinking that interpreting the Bible in new and creative ways—ways maybe that the original author didn't see or intend are faithful to the overall trajectory of the Bible and church tradition—is not disrespectful to the Bible and began to see it as being faithful to it?

What if I told you I think Jesus changed the meaning of his Scriptures too?

YOU HAVE HEARD IT SAID

In one of Jesus' most famous sermons, often called the Sermon on the Mount, he says:

> "Do not think that I have come to abolish the Law or the Prophets; I have not come to abolish them but to fulfill them. For truly I tell you, until heaven and earth disappear, not the smallest letter, not the least stroke of a pen, will by any means disappear from the Law until everything is accomplished. Therefore anyone who sets aside one of the least of these commands and teaches others accordingly will be called least in the kingdom of heaven, but whoever practices and teaches these commands will be called great in the kingdom of heaven. For I tell you that unless your righteousness surpasses that of the Pharisees and the teachers of the law, you will certainly not enter the kingdom of heaven."
>
> *Matthew 5:17–20*

People have wondered for a long time what Jesus meant by this. There are many important (and kind of boring) books written about the history of how people have interpreted these verses. Here's my take: Jesus is about to change the meaning of his Bible.

I was always taught to think about "fulfillment" in the Bible like fortune-telling. Some ancient person predicted something a long time ago, and then Jesus fulfills that prophecy. But it doesn't take much to show that that's not what Matthew means by fulfillment.

In Matthew 2:13–15, the story says an angel showed up to Jesus' pops, Joseph, and told him to take the family down to Egypt because Herod was about to go on a murderous rampage and kill a bunch of babies because he heard one of them was supposed to grow up and become king. Then Matthew says, "So he got up, took the child and his mother during the night and left for Egypt, where he stayed until the death of Herod. And so was fulfilled what the Lord had said through the prophet: 'Out of Egypt I called my son.'"

But if we take two minutes to actually look up what prophetic saying Matthew is referencing, we'll see that "the prophet" wasn't talking about Jesus at all. I mean, it's pretty explicit: "When Israel was a child, I loved him, and out of Egypt I called my son" (Hosea 11:1).

Hosea's "prophecy" was actually looking back to the exodus. What did Hosea *mean*? He meant that a long time ago, God liberated Israel from Egypt. So in what way is Jesus going to Egypt a "fulfillment" of the Bible? Matthew is changing the meaning of the Bible to fit the experiences and circumstances of his day. He has experienced Jesus and is using the language, images, and symbols of the Bible to be faithful to what God is doing in his day. He is saying that Jesus is a New Israel, God's Son in a new way.

So let's keep that in mind when we read the next section of Jesus' sermon:

"You have heard that it was said to the people long ago, 'You shall not murder, and anyone who murders will be subject to judgment.' But I tell you that anyone who is angry with a brother or sister will be subject to judgment.

Again, anyone who says to a brother or sister, 'Raca,' is answerable to the court. And anyone who says, 'You fool!' will be in danger of the fire of hell . . .

"You have heard that it was said, 'You shall not commit adultery.' But I tell you that anyone who looks at a woman lustfully has already committed adultery with her in his heart. If your right eye causes you to stumble, gouge it out and throw it away. It is better for you to lose one part of your body than for your whole body to be thrown into hell. And if your right hand causes you to stumble, cut it off and throw it away. It is better for you to lose one part of your body than for your whole body to go into hell.

"It has been said, 'Anyone who divorces his wife must give her a certificate of divorce.' But I tell you that anyone who divorces his wife, except for sexual immorality, makes her the victim of adultery, and anyone who marries a divorced woman commits adultery.

"Again, you have heard that it was said to the people long ago, 'Do not break your oath, but fulfill to the Lord the vows you have made.' But I tell you, do not swear an oath at all: either by heaven, for it is God's throne; or by the earth, for it is his footstool; or by Jerusalem, for it is the city of the Great King. And do not swear by your head, for you cannot make even one hair white or black. All you need to say is simply 'Yes' or 'No'; anything beyond this comes from the evil one.

"You have heard that it was said, 'Eye for eye, and tooth for tooth.' But I tell you, do not resist an evil person. If anyone slaps you on the right cheek, turn to them the other cheek also. And if anyone wants to sue you and take your shirt, hand over your coat as well. If anyone forces you to go one mile, go with them two miles. Give to the one who asks you, and do not turn away from the one who wants to borrow from you.

"You have heard that it was said, 'Love your neighbor and hate your enemy.' But I tell you, love your enemies and pray for those who persecute you, that you may be children of your Father in heaven. He causes his sun to rise on the evil and the good, and sends rain on the righteous and the unrighteous. If you love those who love you, what reward will you get? Are not even the tax collectors doing that? And if you greet only your own people, what are you doing more than others? Do not even pagans do that? Be perfect, therefore, as your heavenly Father is perfect."

Matthew 5:21–22, 27–48

We are trained to think in either/or statements. *Either* Jesus is saying that the Torah is irrelevant and now we just need to follow Jesus' rules *or* Jesus isn't saying anything new at all and we should try to obey Torah the same way people did a thousand years ago.

Both of these conclusions miss the point. Jesus is not teaching with either/or statements. The "but" in the English translation is misleading. He isn't negating the foundational importance of these earlier sayings and texts; he is showing his respect by updating them for his followers. Or to use our earlier analogy, he is taking the ingredients and putting them together to make a new recipe for his time and in light of his own ministry.

Jesus begins this section by saying that he isn't abolishing the instructions from his forefathers, but is fulfilling them. He then proceeds to quote parts of those instructions and offers a new interpretation for his followers. If you read rabbinic literature, this seems quite common. He's saying, "Let me offer a new interpretation of these texts and ideas based on where we find ourselves today and based on my authority."

What if "fulfilling" Scripture is a creative act where we make new meanings for the Bible based on how we are discerning and experiencing God in our lives and in our culture, thereby keeping it alive and relevant in each generation?

I think every church recognizes the need to do this in some ways. That's why we talk about "applying the Bible to our lives." But most churches are afraid to apply the Bible in any significant way to our current world. We think that throwing in pop culture references is enough updating. But we aren't making any new recipes. We are just putting the same thing together over and over again and calling it something different.

I propose we follow Jesus in more radical ways. To be faithful to the Bible, and to follow in Jesus' "You have heard that it was said . . . But I tell you" footsteps, we have to update our morality, our thinking, our way of being in the world, in light of new facts and understandings we have gained. In this way we are following the Bible, not by keeping to the letter of the law but by keeping to the Spirit. This is partly what I think Paul means in 2 Corinthians 3:3–6 when he compares a life of following engraved letters on "tablets of stone" with "the Spirit": the former kills, but the latter gives life.

If we stick slavishly to letters on a page, we are being like the wicked servant in Jesus' parable about the bags of gold or the less beloved servant in the Jewish story. If we let our fear of "getting it wrong" win, it is as though we are saying we don't trust the Spirit to guide us beyond the letter. It is, after all, the Spirit who Jesus promises will guide us into all truth, not the Bible: "But when he, the Spirit of truth, comes, he will guide you into all the truth. He will not speak on his own; he will speak only what he hears, and he will tell you what is yet to come" (John 16:13).

Is it hard to trust the unseen Spirit of God who resides in each of us and in our communities of faith? Absolutely. And isn't it easier to trust in a book we can memorize and parse to our heart's content? Absolutely. But who said faith was easy?

This is the difference between a Christianity based on a search for certainty through facts and a Christianity based on a search for love through wisdom. For some, searching for certainty through facts is good enough. But for me, it became toxic. My life wasn't either/or. And when I tried to put people into either/or boxes, it turned out I was trying to control them instead of liberate them. It turned out that while I was trying to speak the truth to them in love, I was only telling them my opinion, and it wasn't loving.

THE LAW OF LOVE

When it comes to how to read the Bible through a lens of love, it turns out there is another critical piece to the puzzle. Jesus doesn't leave us completely directionless when it comes to how to reinterpret the Bible.

Jesus is asked 183 questions and only directly answers three.[4] I say this for two reasons. First, I just want everyone to know that when I'm asked really hard questions about the Bible and I deflect, it's not because I don't know or because I'm intimidated by your question; it's because I want to be like Jesus. And I also say this because if Jesus only answers three questions directly, I think it's really important to pay attention to those answers. I want to focus on one in particular.

The pastors of Jesus' day were always trying to trap him with a question. He rarely answers them directly. In Matthew 22, we see three short stories that illustrate these traps. In one story (22:23–33), a group of religious leaders called the Sadducees ask Jesus a pretty ridiculous question about who a woman will be married to in the next life if she's had seven husbands in this life. Why is this a trap? Because the Sadducees were notorious for not believing in the next life. So Jesus answers directly: people aren't going to be married in the next life.

Drat. Foiled again.

Word got out that Jesus owned the Sadducees, so another religious group decided to try to trip up Jesus—this time it was the Pharisees. One of them, an expert in interpreting the Bible, says, "Teacher, which is the greatest commandment in the Law?" Jesus responds directly: "'Love the Lord your God with all your heart and with all your soul and with all your mind.' This is the first and greatest commandment. And the second is like it: 'Love your neighbor as yourself.' All the Law and the Prophets hang on these two commandments" (Matthew 22:36–40).

For me, this becomes the most important interpretive tool we have for how Jesus saw the Scriptures of his day. He quotes two verses from the Old Testament:

- "Love the LORD your God with all your heart and with all your soul and with all your strength" (Deuteronomy 6:5).
- "Do not seek revenge or bear a grudge against anyone among your people, but love your neighbor as yourself" (Leviticus 19:18).

And then he adds something new. Nowhere in the Old Testament does it say that the meaning of the Old Testament depends on these two verses. But Jesus does. *He changes the meaning of these two verses*—and that's significant for us. If we are going to follow Jesus in how we read our Bible, we would be wise to adopt his filter: love.

IF WE ARE GOING TO FOLLOW JESUS IN HOW WE READ OUR BIBLE, WE WOULD BE WISE TO ADOPT HIS FILTER: LOVE.

We saw this in 2 Peter 1:5–8: "For this very reason, make every effort to add to your faith goodness; and to goodness, knowledge; and to knowledge, self-control; and to self-control, perseverance; and to perseverance, godliness; and to godliness, mutual affection; and to mutual affection, love." And again we saw this in 1 Corinthians 13:8, 13: "Love never fails. But where there are prophecies, they will cease; where there are tongues, they will be stilled; where there is knowledge, it will pass away . . . And now these three remain: faith, hope and love. But the greatest of these is love."

We can't let the Bible just stay in the past. We have to update it. It has to make sense to us as we grow in our understanding of science, morality, and technology and as we relate to our current culture. And here Jesus gives us a guide: there are hundreds of ways to interpret the Bible, just make sure all interpretations lead to love.

Everything, and I mean everything, is a tool toward love. If anything takes the place of love, it's an idol. It has taken Jesus' place as the authority in your life. It will take us an entire lifetime to work out what it means for us to love well. But I'd rather spend my time trying to get *that* right than spending my time trying to get the facts right. When Jesus said the Spirit will guide us into all truth, I doubt he meant the Spirit would help us get all our facts right about the mysteries of God and Jesus; I believe he meant the Spirit will guide us as we bump along, fall down, and get back up toward this life of love.

What is the filter we should use to change meaning? Jesus paves the way. Jesus often changes the meanings of ancient traditions in light of a new law—the law of love. Whether it's the pronouncement that "the Sabbath was made for man, not man for the Sabbath" (Mark 2:27) or his famous Torah reversals of "You have heard that it was said . . . But I tell you," we have to take seriously the point Jesus is making: love changes the meaning of our traditions, our experiences, our beliefs, and our reading strategy.

Or as philosopher Jack Caputo summarizes Jesus' ministry, "He kept one thing uppermost in his heart, the love of neighbor and of God, which was unconditional, the sum and substance of the Torah, and he treated everything else, however sacred it was in men's eyes, as man made, conditional, flexible, deconstructible. His periodic flashes of anger are reserved for those who confused the latter with the former."[5]

GRACE FOR US, JUDGMENT FOR THEM

It turns out it's not just Jesus we find changing the meaning of God's Word. Seems like love even changes God's mind about God's Word.

We looked briefly at the story of the golden calf, but we skipped one curious part. Moses went up the mountain and wasn't seen or heard from for forty days. After such a long time, the people assumed God killed Moses, so they asked Aaron to take up the mantle of leadership. But this time they wanted Yahweh not to be so scary or unpredictable, so instead of letting God decide how God will show up, they created a golden calf and called it God. I mean, Moses was a good guy and all, but hey, the show must go on.

Meanwhile, back on Sinai, I assume God's eyes were rolling and the sighs of annoyance were audible. "'I have seen these people,' the LORD said to Moses, 'and they are a stiff-necked people. Now leave me alone so that my anger may burn against them and that I may destroy them. Then I will make you into a great nation'" (Exodus 32:9–10).

I like to use this line on my wife when my daughter insists on not listening to me and doing things her own way. "I have seen these kids," Jared says to Sarah, "and they are a stiff-necked people. Now leave me alone so that my anger may burn against them and that I may destroy them." Like I said, I take the Bible seriously and want to be like God when I grow up.

Back to the Bible though. According to this passage, God intended to destroy the Israelites.

Moses reminded God of the promises he had made, and God's mind was changed. God had said, "Leave me alone and let me destroy these people," but after talking to Moses, God said, "The LORD, the LORD, the compassionate and gracious God, slow to anger, abounding in love and faithfulness, maintaining love to thousands, and forgiving wickedness, rebellion and sin" (Exodus 34:6–7).

Israel celebrated how gracious God had been to them over the years. Even though the Israelites were a "stiff-necked people," God kept changing God's mind about them. Over and over there were pronouncements about God's judgment that would get postponed because of God's love.

In 722 BCE, the Assyrians wiped out the northern nation of Israel, leaving only the southern nation of Judah to carry on the legacy of the Israelite religion and culture. The capital of Assyria was Nineveh. Yes, that Nineveh. It is against this backdrop we must read the famous story of Jonah and his unfortunate Pinocchio experience with a giant fish. This is another example of how believing that the most important aspect of the Bible is the facts can lead to missing the point of most of the Bible.

In Jonah 3:4, God's words are clear: "Forty more days and Nineveh will be overthrown." And then, similar to what we see in Exodus 34, God's mind is changed because the Ninevites repent, and God spares the Ninevites (Jonah 3:10).

What's interesting here is Jonah's response. It's all fun and games until God's love starts changing God's judgment toward people we think of as enemies. The Bible says God's grace seemed "very wrong" to Jonah (4:1), and he prayed to God, "Isn't this what I said, LORD, when I was still at home? That is what I tried to forestall by fleeing to Tarshish. I knew that you are a gracious and compassionate God, slow to anger and abounding in love, a God who relents from sending calamity. Now, LORD, take away my life, for it is better for me to die than to live" (Jonah 4:2–3).

This is a powerful story that gets at the core of what it means to let love be our guide when we read the Bible. The real problem with "speaking the truth in love" is that at the end of the day, we want grace for ourselves and judgment for other people. It's important that we "don't compromise the truth" when we are looking at other people, but it suddenly becomes more important that we "show grace and love" when we are looking at ourselves or our own tribe. Jonah is a damning parable about how ugly it looks when self-righteousness gets masked as justice and truth gets ripped from the context of love. Truth telling is always in service to love and should never be an excuse for judgment.[6]

CHAPTER SEVEN

LOVE CHANGES THE TRUTH

You know where I'm going with this. If love has changed God's mind and Jesus changes the meaning of the Bible because of love, we should be open to the same. Perhaps love should change our minds and our beliefs. Perhaps love should change how we read the Bible. These ideas may cause you some anxiety. They did for me. I like rules and black-and-white instructions.

Ask my wife. In our twenties, some of our biggest fights had to do with following instructions. Nothing gave me more anxiety than watching in terror, helplessly, as my wife would throw the instructions of a new device to the side while she pushed random buttons and said to herself, *I wonder what this does.* Even now, my palms get sweaty thinking about it. Thanks for making me relive the trauma.

In all honesty though, the older I get, the more I realize that life isn't black-and-white. Rules that were meant for good, if applied in a wooden way, can actually cause harm. Life experience has put me in many situations where I'm stuck wondering whether to follow the letter of a law or use the spirit of the law. Learning when to follow the letter and when to break the letter and follow the spirit is what we call wisdom. Looking back, not one time did my wife's way of learning a new piece of technology lead to any disasters. Her way was faster and more fun, and it led to discovering features I never would have known were there.

I think Jesus, Matthew, Paul, and many of the other writers of the New Testament were more like my wife than I want to admit. They were facing new situations and circumstances. The old instructions were a great starting place, but this was new. They had to figure out how to make *new* meaning from old texts. So if we ask ourselves, "What would Jesus do?" we have to admit we might need to learn how to change the meaning of the Bible too.

When I first had this thought, I wondered, *Who am I though? Sure, God and Jesus have the authority to change the meaning of the Bible, but* me? Then one day I was reading the gospel of John and came upon a few passages that changed my mind.

After a little introduction, John jumps right into Jesus' ministry in chapters 2–12. Jesus has been providing food and wine in miraculous ways, walking on water, healing the sick, and even raising Lazarus from the dead in a climactic moment in John 11. This last act was the tipping point for the religious leaders—he was getting too popular among the people, and he had to go. The next time we see Jesus in public, he will be arrested. But between the resurrection of Lazarus and his arrest (John 13–17), we get an intimate look at what Jesus says to his disciples with death at his doorstep. He begins to comfort his disciples. It's one of the very few places in all of Scripture where Jesus himself tells us what to expect after his death.

He says in this section:

> "Believe me when I say that I am in the Father and the Father is in me; or at least believe on the evidence of the works themselves. Very truly I tell you, whoever believes in me will do the works I have been doing, and they will do even greater things than these, because I am going to the Father."
>
> *John 14:11–12*

> "But very truly I tell you, it is for your good that I am going away. Unless I go away, the Advocate will not come to you; but if I go, I will send him to you . . . I have much more to say to you, more than you can now bear. But when he, the Spirit of truth, comes, he will guide you into all the truth."
>
> *John 16:7, 12–13*

These two passages were life-giving to me. Or maybe it's better to say permission-giving. Sometimes we can feel like all the people back in Bible times were somehow inherently more spiritual than us. But here in John, Jesus paints a different picture. When Jesus leaves, he tells us that he will provide the Spirit of God, who does two radical things: allows us to do even greater things than Jesus and guides us into all truth.

I take this to mean, "You can't stay still. Keep moving forward. Go find more of God's truth in the world, just as I have done. And don't worry, the Spirit will guide you." Notice what Jesus didn't say. He didn't say that the Bible would guide you into all truth; he said the Spirit would.

Just like we saw in the parable of the traveling master we talked about earlier, staying put and creating nothing new isn't how we respect the Spirit of God. What we thought was humility is actually disrespect. The Spirit of God who was hovering over the face of the waters all the way back in Genesis 1 as an agent of creation is still teeming with life. That same Spirit guided the church through the Roman Empire, through the Middle Ages, through scientific breakthroughs, through the discovery of evolution, and even through the height of reality TV.

Perhaps it's time we recognize the power of the Spirit to teach us *new* things. The very metaphor of the guide means that the Spirit is taking us into uncharted territory. We must carry on the legacy of Jesus, Paul, Matthew, and all the biblical writers by trusting the Spirit to guide us into *new* truths about God.

ROOTS AND FRUITS

Jesus' formula, "You have heard that it was said . . . But I tell you," is very important. He doesn't erase what we heard before. He doesn't hide it and say, "This is what the Bible *really* meant, you silly folks." He says, "I know what you've heard. I've heard it too. But I'm building off that and going into uncharted territory." This is the best model for biblical interpretation—being firmly grounded in the roots of our tradition and yet growing new fruit in each season. It is important to begin with "You have heard that it was said" and find ourselves rooted in the Bible. It's *just as important* that we don't stop there. In each season and each generation, we have to add our own "But I tell you," adding the fruit for our season. What we have heard is important, but love matters more. And that's the creative work we have to undertake in our time and in our day.

According to Jesus, the focus should be on the fruit, not on proving to the other people at our church that we know our roots. The point of reading the Bible is to produce good fruit, not to brag to people about how much we read the Bible.

In Matthew 7:15–20, Jesus says this about false prophets: "Watch out for false prophets. They come to you in sheep's clothing, but inwardly they are ferocious wolves. By their fruit you will recognize them. Do people pick grapes from thorn-bushes, or figs from thistles? Likewise, every good tree bears good fruit, but a bad tree bears bad fruit. A good tree cannot bear bad fruit, and a bad tree cannot bear good fruit. Every tree that does not bear good fruit is cut down and thrown into the fire. Thus, by their fruit you will recognize them." Another way of saying this, when it comes to the Bible, is that Christian practice isn't about simply *discovering* what's "really" there.

In many of the churches I've attended, or even pastored, we were trying so hard to be respectful to the Bible and to be relevant to our current day and culture. But because we couldn't imagine being okay with changing the meaning of the Bible, we labored over ways to fit Paul into our current cultural climate and called it "discovering what Paul *really meant*." We ended up erasing Paul instead of being in conversation with Paul. It's awfully arrogant to think that after two thousand years, we'd finally "gotten Paul right." But we paraded our own ethics around and erased Paul's voice—pretending that our ethics are the same as Paul's.

I've come to learn that we must let Paul be Paul, let us be us, and let us trust that the Spirit of God who was at work in Paul's day is still at work in us today. Truth will be found in the conversation between Paul, us, and anyone else who is trying desperately to find out what it means to love well in this world.

For example, when I was growing up, it was clear biblical teaching that women shouldn't be in positions of authority over men. This was, of course, taken directly from 1 Timothy 2:11–14, which reads, "A woman should learn in quietness and full submission. I do not permit a woman to teach or to assume authority over a man; she must be quiet. For Adam was formed first, then Eve. And Adam was not the one deceived; it was the woman who was deceived and became a sinner."

While this may be the most explicit biblical passage on this topic, there were also other biblical reasons given for why women shouldn't be pastors. There is also clear priority of men in leadership throughout the Old Testament, as well as in the household codes of Ephesians 5, Colossians 3, and 1 Peter 3. To tie it all together, there is an implicit connection between the hierarchy of the household and the hierarchy of the church (1 Timothy 3:4; Titus 1:6).[1]

In 1960, 2.3 percent of clergy were women.[2] In 2018, that number had risen to 27 percent and continues to climb.[3] In the United Kingdom as of July 2012, 20 percent of all ministers were women, and 71 percent of evangelicals in the UK agreed that women should be eligible for the same roles in the church as men.[4]

What has changed since 1960? Have people gotten better at Bible study? Did biblical scholars make some great "discovery" since 1960? Have archaeologists uncovered some wonderful historical fact that has changed our minds? Do we now understand what Paul *really* meant in his letter to Timothy?

I would suggest not. I would suggest that as we recognize that "separate but equal" doesn't work and that there have been centuries of male-dominated social and political systems, we also recognize that maybe it's not loving to tell women they aren't allowed to be in certain positions simply because they are women. As the Spirit of God has guided us, we have come to new realizations and truths about what it means to be human.

And as we come to those realizations, we start to emphasize certain parts of our Bible and minimize others. We start to use our wisdom to discern where to follow the letter of the law and where to follow the Spirit.

So instead of 1 Timothy 2:11–14 or Colossians 3:8 becoming our standard, we lean more on verses like Galatians 3:28: "There is neither Jew nor Gentile, neither slave nor free, nor is there male and female, for you are all one in Christ Jesus."

You have heard that it was said that women shall not have authority over men. But we tell you there is neither male nor female, for we are all one in Christ Jesus.

If we go back another hundred years, we see a similar change in beliefs about slavery. The Old Testament doesn't condemn slavery. Frankly, neither does the New Testament—not outright. Paul writes in Ephesians 6:5–8:

> Slaves, obey your earthly masters with respect and fear, and with sincerity of heart, just as you would obey Christ. Obey them not only to win their favor when their eye is on you, but as slaves of Christ, doing the will of God from your heart. Serve wholeheartedly, as if you were

serving the Lord, not people, because you know that the Lord will reward each one for whatever good they do, whether they are slave or free.

The abolitionists admitted that if you go by the letter of the Bible, slavery would be permitted. Fortunately, the Spirit of God convicted them otherwise, and by rooting themselves in the spirit of the Bible, not just the letter, they created new meaning. Instead of leaning on what many would call the "plain interpretation" of Ephesians 6:5–8, they leaned more on the story of the slave Onesimus, found in Philemon, and on Colossians 3:11, which reads, "Here there is no Gentile or Jew, circumcised or uncircumcised, barbarian, Scythian, slave or free, but Christ is all, and is in all."

That Spirit of Jesus, the One whose first sermon was about setting the prisoners free, overshadowed Paul's context in Ephesians 6, because as we have established, where the Spirit of the Lord is, there is freedom (2 Corinthians 3:17).

You have heard that it was said that slaves should obey their masters. But we tell you there is neither slave nor free, but Christ is all, and is in all.

How can Christians, who all confess to the authority of the Bible, come to opposite conclusions from the same book? Because the Bible is diverse, it emphasizes different things. As we've already discovered, the New Testament itself changes the meaning of the Old Testament. The Bible invites us to wisdom because it reflects life: ambiguous, diverse, and open to different meanings.

My suspicion is that the Spirit of God is working in a similar way when it comes to the church's understanding and acceptance of LGBTQ neighbors. Just as our ethics rightly shifted away from opposing women's equality and endorsing slavery—shifting the lens through which we read the Bible—a similar shift may be happening with regard to how people think about LGBTQ relationships. From 2007 to 2015, Christian acceptance of homosexuality in society rose from 44 percent to 54 percent. That includes 51 percent of evangelical millennials.[5] And that was five years ago! Many religious groups now support same-sex marriage, including 66 percent of white mainline Protestants and 61 percent of Catholics.[6]

The Spirit of God is on the move again. My experiences with gay Christians have been very similar to Peter's vision in Acts 10 about clean and unclean foods. In the Old Testament, the Bible was very clear about clean and unclean foods. Getting your diet wrong was a sin.[7] It was black-and-white. Then Jesus showed up in a vision where Peter saw all these unclean animals come marching in, and Jesus said, "Get up, Peter. Kill and eat." Peter was appalled. Peter resisted Jesus because of his tradition and what the Scriptures clearly said.

I'm sure many thoughts were racing through Peter's head. *This can't be. I'm probably just compromising with the culture. What will people think? They'll think I'm just caving to that new saying, 'When in Rome . . .' I'll probably lose my position as a leader in this new movement.* I mean, the vision came only to Peter and to no one else. How would he explain to people that the dietary laws his people followed for the past several hundred years were no longer important? Who would believe him?

We aren't sure what he was thinking, but according to Acts 10, he said back to Jesus, "Surely not, Lord!" followed by, "I have never eaten anything impure or unclean." Then the voice spoke back, "Do not call anything impure that God has made clean."

Now that itself shows us something powerful about how Jesus can work. Jesus changes the meaning of the dietary laws in the Old Testament. Peter, who had a history of telling Jesus what we're "supposed to do," was put in his place. "Do not call anything impure that God has made clean."

But that's not the end of the story. It gets more personal. The text goes on to say that "while Peter was wondering about the meaning of the vision," three men came to him. That's a clue that maybe the point of the vision isn't just about food. What else could it mean? Well, the story will tell us.

These men were there to invite Peter to a Gentile's house— someone named Cornelius:

> As Peter entered the house, Cornelius met him and fell at his feet in reverence. But Peter made him get up. "Stand up," he said, "I am only a man myself."
>
> While talking with him, Peter went inside and found a large gathering of people. He said to them: "You are well aware that it is against our law for a Jew to associate with or visit a Gentile. But God has shown me that I should not call anyone impure or unclean. So when I was sent for, I came without raising any objection. May I ask why you sent for me?"
>
> *Acts 10:25–29*

Did you catch that? Jesus showed Peter a bunch of unclean animals and told him to eat them. Sure, maybe it meant that those old food laws didn't apply anymore. But that's not what Peter got out of it. He said, "God has shown me that I should not call *anyone* impure or unclean." Peter had determined that the meaning of the vision wasn't about food but about people.

Then the Spirit of God descended on everyone present, even the Gentiles. "Then Peter said, 'Surely no one can stand in the way of their being baptized with water. They have received the Holy Spirit just as we have.' So he ordered that they be baptized in the name of Jesus Christ" (Acts 10:46–48).

For me personally, I have experienced too many Spirit-filled gay Christians to deny their baptism.

You have heard that it was said that man should not lie with another man; it is an abomination. But we tell you God has shown us that we should not call anyone impure or unclean. No one is an abomination. Surely no one can stand in the way of their being baptized with water. They have received the Holy Spirit just as we have.

These changes in our interpretation can be explained in a few ways. Either the "true" meaning of these passages has been hidden for centuries and we are just now discovering it, or we have to wrestle with what the Bible means in light of how we are growing in wisdom as a church through experience and learning from science, psychology, sociology, and how we are discerning the movement of the Spirit of God.[8] We must update what the Bible means in light of our best interpretation of love that we have available to us at the time. This is what it means to be faithful to the Bible, to a life of wisdom and of following Jesus, who did the same thing and who tells us that the sum total of all laws is a life of wisdom directed toward love of God, love of neighbor, and love of self.

JUST PLAY

Does this mean we can change the Bible to mean whatever we want it to as long as we can justify it as loving? This reminds me of a great conversation between Alice and Humpty Dumpty in Lewis Carroll's *Through the Looking Glass*:

> "When *I* use a word," Humpty Dumpty said, in rather a scornful tone, "it means just what I choose it to mean—neither more nor less."
>
> "The question is," said Alice, "whether you *can* make words mean so many different things."
>
> "The question is," said Humpty Dumpty, "which is to be master—that's all."[9]

This is how it feels: Who is master when it comes to meaning? As we mentioned, meaning-truth is found in relationship with people. It's a conversation. Asking who is to be master is to miss the conversation altogether. It is that perfectionist thinking rearing its head once again. If you are asking about where meaning resides—*With the original writer? With me individually? With the church broadly? With my community of faith?*—the answer is yes!

We are all in the conversation together, and it is *true love* that guards us from making the Bible mean whatever we want. It is out of deep respect for our conversation partners that we find meaning. As scholar Hans-Georg Gadamer wrote, "Words do not 'stand' on their own account. Whether they are spoken or written, their meaning is only fully realized within the context of life."[10] Joseph Gordon applies this to the Bible in particular: "Whatever 'it' [meaning, the Bible] is in the concrete, its authority and meaning depend upon its use, and its use has varied throughout Christian history and is enormously varied in contemporary Christianity communities."[11]

WE ARE ALL IN THE CONVERSATION TOGETHER, AND IT IS TRUE LOVE THAT GUARDS US FROM MAKING THE BIBLE MEAN WHATEVER WE WANT.

The Bible will always require a conversation partner to make meaning of it. Some conversation partners will inevitably find certain passages more significant than others. Those other readers may resonate with certain passages differently than those with a different context and background. There will always be more meaning than what the book itself can contain.

In other words, we don't have the problem of a Bible that becomes meaningless as more and more generations pass; we have a better problem. We have a Bible that contains an abundance of meaning!

As long as we use love to guard us from disrespecting the original authors, as long as we use love to guard us from interpreting the Bible to oppress instead of liberate, as long as we use love to show grace to those with different perspectives, we can find freedom in the way we read the Bible. We need not worry about not having enough degrees to read it accurately.

We will always be growing in our desire to understand the original language and context out of our love for our original conversation partners. We need not worry about not having enough knowledge. We will always remember that it is, after all, a tool on the path to true love.

Charlie Parker was one of the greatest jazz musicians of all time. He was particularly good at a style of jazz called improvisation, which is a great picture of what I believe biblical interpretation is all about. Without a good understanding of improv, it can seem lazy—you're not disciplined enough to master the music on the page, so you just "make it up." But that's not a correct understanding of improv. It takes incredible skill and respect for the art form to be able to go "off script" and make beautiful music without knowing where it will take you.

Any improvisational artist, whether performing in comedy or music, will tell you it takes deep respect and understanding of the art form to be able to go beyond it. A quote often attributed to Charlie Parker has guided my Bible reading for about a decade now. When asked how to become a great improv musician, he supposedly said, "Master your instrument, master the music, and then forget all that bullshit and just play."[12]

Of course, I don't know if Charlie ever actually said it. But it means a lot to me. For me, this statement mirrors Jesus' formula of "You have heard that it was said . . . But I tell you."

MASTER THE MUSIC

Our music is the Bible. If we hope to go beyond the Bible, we must first root ourselves in it. If we are going to create *new meaning* out of what the Bible says, we'd better know *what* it says. If you want a starting point, I encourage you to read books by Jewish scholars like Jon Levenson or James Kugel. Or if you want a shortcut, listen to Levenson's interview with us on the podcast I cohost, *The Bible for Normal People.*[13] He seamlessly weaves narratives and biblical passages into his conversation in a way that shows that the Bible is part of him. Some people say you know you've become proficient in a language if you dream in that language. I have a feeling that Levenson dreams in Bible.

The root of Bible interpretation is understanding what the original authors intended. However, as I mentioned earlier, there is a problem. We can't just go ask the authors, since they are all dead. So we rely on context to help us—both literary and historical context.

This is where we can learn to rely on biblical scholarship. Just like natural scientists have developed a reliable process for coming to scientific truths, scholars are constantly refining their processes and methods for trying to determine authorial intent and the original meaning of biblical texts. Scholars work to figure out which tools will help us better understand the world in which the Bible was written. As in any good relationship, we need to understand what Paul was trying to communicate before we go beyond Paul.

Another way of thinking about it: if we do not take very seriously the first part of Jesus' formula, "You have heard that it was said," we disrespect the text and show that we aren't interested in a relationship with the Bible but are only interested in hearing ourselves talk, only interested in confirming what we already think.

As in any good relationship, we show our respect by listening first. So take some time to listen to the music. Read the Bible. Ask questions. Learn about the context. Find a sense of wonder. If we want the Bible to be meaningful to us, we have to put in the work to try to understand it. Just as in any relationship, we won't ever arrive. We won't ever understand it perfectly. But the relationship is in the striving to understand. However, just as in other relationships, we need to understand more than just the author's intention to have the Bible be meaningful to us; we need to understand ourselves.

MASTER THE INSTRUMENT

Our instrument is comprised of the filters we use to read and interpret the Bible. It is important to ask, "How am I deciding what this means?" We all interpret the Bible. We all use filters. The point isn't to pretend we can get rid of our filters and just "read the Bible as it is." That would be impossible. And since meaning is vital to being human, I would also point out that it's not even desirable. The point is to become aware of our filters and decide which ones are better than others.

Mastering our "instrument"—understanding our interpretative filters—is about our emotional intelligence, our ethical and moral frameworks, our personalities, our bodies, our cultural and social experiences. It's about becoming aware of how all these filters inform how we act every day and then striving to adjust, based on love. In a word, our instrument is *wisdom*. When we are reading Paul in the Bible, we want to be good conversation partners. The goal is not to get rid of Paul, but neither is the goal to get rid of us.

When we use good interpretive tools, Paul will sometimes challenge us, and we will say, "Paul is right. I need to allow his words to criticize how I think about the world." And other times, when we come to clarity about how we think about the world through our own experiences, we may find ourselves saying to Paul, "You have heard it that it was said . . . But I tell you."

On an early episode of *The Bible for Normal People*, we interviewed the Catholic friar Richard Rohr. On that show, he discussed a similar idea to filters. He compared Christian faith to a tricycle, saying we are guided by three wheels—experience, tradition, and the Bible. However, for Rohr, the front wheel is experience. Why? Because it is through our experience that we understand our tradition and the Bible. When I was in seminary, I spent hundreds of hours learning about my tradition and how it interacted with the Bible. I spent hundreds of hours learning about the Bible. But I spent approximately zero hours learning about my filters—my personality, my strengths and weaknesses, my emotional health, how my culture impacts how I read my Bible. That's like learning to read music but never picking up an instrument—and then expecting to play a beautiful song.

For almost all of church history, faith rested on more than the Bible for all the obvious reasons stated above. And each of those things—experience, tradition, and the Bible—needs to *inform* the others. In other words, sometimes our traditions need to shape our experiences. Sometimes the Bible needs to shape our experiences. And sometimes our experiences need to change our interpretation of the Bible. And so our reading of the Bible needs to be influenced and informed by our experiences and our traditions.

I in no way pretend to be smarter than Richard Rohr, but I would humbly add another filter to the life of faith, namely, community. While some may see community as a subset of our experience, I think it's important enough to separate, because our culture tends to be individualistic and because our community is so influential to how we see the world. We are shaped by the people around us and the culture we find ourselves in, and they also impact the life of faith. In fact, I would say learning to lean into our communities is central to the life of wisdom—to mastering our instrument. So we are on a lifelong journey to understand, both in themselves and in how they relate to one another, these four things: ourselves (our experiences), tradition, community, and the Bible.

But I'll emphasize it again. It's so important that we spend as much time learning our filters as we do the Bible. That is how we master the instrument we use to play the music. We are rooted in the Bible, and then we are faithful to it by going beyond it. If we don't understand our filters well, we run the risk of being unaware of how our unhealthy view of ourselves or our community or our tradition is affecting how we read the Bible.

Learning how to reinterpret the Bible can feel overwhelming or daunting. If you feel like you'll never learn enough to be able to do that, I would suggest that's your perfectionist talking again. No one ever said you had to know it all to use it. There is no musician who has mastered the music perfectly. There is no Bible scholar who has mastered all the areas of biblical studies perfectly. You're mistaking the tool for the goal again. It's a journey of discovery. We're all in a process as we learn to be in relationship with the Bible. Is mastering the music important?

Yes. Is mastering the instrument important? Yes. But let's not forget the goal: *just play.* In other words, love matters more.

WHEN IN DOUBT, SEEK LOVE

Saint Augustine of Hippo, one of the most famous saints in the history of the church, was apparently listening to Jesus. To be fair, I think Augustine also got a lot of things wrong. But he lived seventeen hundred years ago and was trying his best to figure out what all this Christianity stuff meant without the hindsight of almost two thousand years of church tradition, like we have today. So cut him some slack and stop judging him.

Anyway, Augustine wrote a massive set of books on how to interpret the Bible. Not to spoil it, since I'm sure you're already on Amazon to order it, but I'll give you a hint: he didn't read the Bible literally.

However, he did understand that the Bible is complicated. So, following Jesus' lead, he gave us a very helpful tool:

> Whoever, then, thinks that he understands the Holy Scriptures, or any part of them, but puts such an interpretation upon them as does not tend to build up this twofold love of God and our neighbor, does not yet understand them as he ought. If on the other hand a man draws a meaning from them that may be used for the building up of love, even though he does not happen upon the precise meaning which the author whom he reads intended to express in that place, he is not pernicious, and he is wholly clear from the charge of deception.[14]

In other words, if a passage from the Bible is ambiguous, the best interpretation is whatever leads us to love better. The proper goal of reading our Bibles isn't to get it right; it's to love. Yes, thinking deeply about theology and how to interpret the Bible is important. But love matters more. I often find myself in Christian circles where the person who spends the most time reading the Bible is considered the godliest. That's like saying the singer who reads sheet music most is the best singer. Or as the John Craigie chorus goes, "Oh, you're doing it wrong, dissecting the bird, trying to find the song. It's a miracle that you're here at all."[15]

I was having coffee with a friend a decade or so ago, and she confessed she hadn't been reading her Bible much because she had been busy taking trips to foreign countries to help build houses for the underprivileged. She said some of her friends had been giving her a hard time because she hadn't been having a regular devotional time to study Scripture. I wanted to shake her. But I refrained. Instead, I gently asked why we read Scripture. "So we know how to live like a Christian," was her response. Then I not so gently suggested that actually living like a Christian was probably more important than reading a book that told her how to live like a Christian. I suggested her guilt was unfounded and encouraged her to find satisfaction in the treasure, not the map.

THE BIBLICAL AUTOPSY

As I mentioned before when I embarrassingly admitted my appreciation for Nic Cage, I live near Philadelphia, where things are just old. We have a lot of America's firsts. We boast the first public library, first mint, first zoo, first world's fair, and, most importantly, first Girl Scout Cookie sale. We also boast the first hospital and the first medical school.

When you take a tour of Pennsylvania Hospital, founded in 1751, you walk into a room that looks like a circular courtroom. There are a few rows of benches on the ground level, and then a balcony with a few rows of seats—all surrounding a singular wooden bed that sits in the center. This room is called the surgical amphitheatre, where doctors performed public surgeries from 11:00 a.m. to 2:00 p.m. on sunny days (since there was no electricity). Of course, these surgeries fell quickly out of favor once doctors realized that clean rooms without random people's germs helped patients not die. However, for many years, you could stroll into the amphitheatre on a weekday at noon and watch a doctor conduct his work. If you happened to be alive between 1804 and the 1830s, you might have had the special privilege of watching a surgery happen before the use of any anesthesia.[16]

I paint this picture because doctors also regularly performed autopsies in that room for the public to see. People were eager to see a doctor dissect a human body and identify all the different pieces.

This is, unfortunately, too perfect of an analogy for how some people think of church. We all sit on our benches as we watch the pastor-doctor stand over the wooden lectern to perform a public autopsy on the Bible. He (too often it has been a he) pulls out his tools of Bible study, looks sternly at the dead body in front of him, and starts to pull things out and pronounce to his awestruck audience what they mean.

THE BIBLE IS A COMPOST PILE

Rather than seeing the Bible as a dead body that undergoes a weekly autopsy, I prefer seeing the Bible as a pile of compost. I get this image from the noted biblical scholar Walter Brueggemann in his book *Texts under Negotiation*:

> The Bible is the *compost pile* that provides material for new life. I do not use this figure as an irreverent metaphor to suggest that the Bible is "garbage." Rather, I use it to suggest that the Bible itself is not the actual place of new growth. Our present life, when we undertake new growth, is often inadequate, arid, or even barren. It needs to be enriched, and for that enrichment, we go back to the deposits of old growth that have been discarded, but that continue to ferment and may contain resources for a way to new life.[17]

The interesting thing about a compost pile is that unless you plant something in it, it's just a pile of garbage. But if you do plant something, it becomes the necessary grounding and foundation for something new and beautiful to grow out of it.

Without the compost, a seed is useless. And without the seed, the compost is useless. Each finds significance and meaning in connection to the other. When we find ourselves rooted in the Bible rather than disrespecting it by either making it mean whatever we want it to or by not making it mean anything new, we find ourselves growing in new ways.

I don't know of anyone who just "makes the Bible mean whatever they want it to." Every act of creating something new is simply bringing to light in a new way something that was always there, perhaps implicit or perhaps just unnoticed because without a new context it couldn't be noticed. Just as the compost and the seed need each other, so it is with the Bible and modern readers. We can't make it mean whatever we want it to, but if we listen closely enough, and if we root ourselves in it deeply enough, it can mean many more things than we thought.

CHAPTER EIGHT

SPEAKING THE TRUTH IN LOVE

L ove has a way of changing our minds about what is true. It doesn't change the facts, of course. It changes what the facts mean and leads us to wisdom. It changes how we see the world. And if we get enough people to change how they see the world, it changes the world. It is true in science, and it is true in the church.

It can be a good and beautiful thing to change our minds about what is true in light of how we experience the world through the lens of love. But when fear or a need to control (which, let's be honest, is usually also fear) is the lens we use to filter our experience of the world, we start to prioritize defending our opinions above loving our neighbor, and the system gets short-circuited. As we've already seen, truth is a tool. It can be used to build up or tear down, to heal or to harm. If our idea of truth doesn't include prioritizing love, if it's just about facts, it isn't true in the broader sense. Or at the very least, it isn't Christian.

For some reason, in my experience, when the phrase "speaking the truth in love" is used, rarely does the person hearing it feel loved. Instead, it's most often used as a way to convince someone that they are being loved even when it doesn't feel that way. It's not often used of someone heavily invested in colaboring with someone in their struggle, but as a way to lob hurtful opinions, walk away, and feel guilt-free.

In the winter of 2019, the Methodist Church, which represents more than twelve million Christians in America, met in St. Louis for their General Conference. In a special session, they voted to condemn same-sex marriages and gay clergy. In one presentation before the vote, Nancy Denardo, a lay delegate from the western part of Pennsylvania, said this in defense of that Traditional Plan:

> Galatians 6:1: "Brothers and sisters, if someone is caught in a sin, you who are spiritual should restore him gently. But watch yourself as you also may be tempted." And in verse 7: "Do not be deceived, God cannot be mocked. A person reaps what they sow."
>
> Friends, please stop sowing seeds of deceit. The word became flesh. Not the flesh becomes the word. I'm truly sorry if the truth of the gospel hurts anyone. But know that I, and those who support the Traditional Plan, love you enough to tell you the truth. God gives you free will, choose wisely, choose God's true words.[1]

Let me be clear. I firmly believe Ms. Denardo wants to love her neighbor as herself. I assume her heart is in the right place. I am not trying to pick on her. But her words are an example of the beliefs that seem to be behind the use of the phrase "speaking the truth in love" by many people.

"BOTH ARE THE WORDS OF THE LIVING GOD"

How the phrase "speaking the truth in love" is used above reveals the assumption that God's Word and my opinion about the interpretation of are the same thing. For some, this may be a lack of humility, and for others, just a simple mistake. Either way, instead of wrestling and discerning together, recognizing that both "sides" are doing their best but at the end of the day are simply giving their opinion, people have already concluded that God is on their side. So this isn't a conversation toward mutual understanding but a choice: accept my interpretation or go against God's Word.

Instead, what might it look like to begin with love and inclusion as the foundation for our disagreements? What might it look like to keep our personal convictions without wielding those opinions in a way that those who are being talked about will feel excluded from the community? To redeem this phrase, "speaking the truth in love," is to recognize we could be wrong in our interpretation. It is to advocate for the "perhaps." In a world that idolizes certainty, I inject "perhaps." It is in the space between "I know" and "I don't know" that we find relationship and growth.

It is a place of proper humility, this "perhaps." It doesn't say, "I am an idiot." Nor does it say, "You are an idiot." It says, "Let's talk further because perhaps you are right. Or perhaps I am."

IT IS IN THE SPACE BETWEEN "I KNOW" AND "I DON'T KNOW" THAT WE FIND RELATIONSHIP AND GROWTH.

There's a great story in the Jewish Talmud about two schools that disagreed about "God's true words":

> For three years there was a dispute between the school of Shammai and the school of Hillel, the ones asserting, "The law is according to our views," and the others asserting, "The law is according to our views." Then a divine voice came forth and said, "The utterances of the one and those of the other are both the words of the living God, but the law is according to the school of Hillel."
>
> But since both are the words of the living God, what entitled the school of Hillel to have the law fixed according to their rulings? Because they were kindly and humble; they taught their own rulings as well as those of the school of Shammai.[2]

What's going on here? Well, two groups of people are arguing about who has the right interpretation of the Bible. And a voice from heaven comes down to say, "The Bible could be taken either way—it's ambiguous. So the winner, the group with the right interpretation, is the group that argued for their views with kindness and humility and wasn't afraid to teach both sides."

Sometimes getting it right isn't about knowing the facts, but about humility and respecting other people's opinions. In other words, getting it right is about loving well.

We often use the phrase "speaking the truth in love" because we believe that people change when we tell them they are sinning and living their life wrong. As we saw earlier, the change paradox, and most of our personal experiences as well, tells us that's a flawed tactic. If we are truly interested in transforming someone else's life, it won't happen by sharing our unwarranted opinion.

I wonder if many of us truly do believe that love includes standing by our opinion of someone's life choices. There are some classic examples that people use to defend this view. For example, if you were about to take poison, wouldn't you want someone to come and tell you they're sure it's poison and warn you against taking it? Wouldn't it be loving to tell them? Sure. But would it be loving to keep telling them several times, even though they are grown adults and have decided for themselves that it's not poison and have taken the drink again and again and not died? No, I would call that coercive and disrespectful. We must respect people's choices.

But there is something even deeper going on in my experi ence when someone says they are simply "speaking the truth in love."

I was talking with a family once who began to share what they thought about people who were gay. One of the women asked a young man whose wife had just had their first baby, "What would you do if your son grew up and was gay?" This man, whom I had only ever experienced as friendly, gentle, and respectful, became angry, and his hands started to shake as he said, "I'd kick his ass." His discomfort was palpable. This seems different from simply telling someone they are about to take poison, if that was his opinion. He was disgusted by the idea that his child might be gay—disgusted enough to threaten violence. I have no doubt that if his son ever were to come out to him, his disgust would be unleashed, and he would call it "speaking the truth in love."

May we not confuse our discomfort with our conscience. May we not justify our discomfort by calling it "standing up for truth." I have plenty of people who love me well, even if we disagree on some fundamental beliefs, to know that love can shine through difference.

This has been my greatest sadness—that we hide our disgust, discomfort, and anger behind a veil of innocence called "just wanting to save people from pain, wanting to speak the truth in love." People aren't dumb. The discomfort and hatred will be felt, even if the words out of our mouths are, "I'm just telling you this because I love you."

A recent Pew Research Center survey shows that most Americans believe the way we talk about politics has gotten worse. A whopping 85 percent of U.S. adults say our conversations have become more negative and less respectful.[3]

Part of what it means for love to matter more is to worry less about convincing people we are right, including being right about our political positions, and to work toward regaining some of those "Hillel" virtues such as kindness and humility.

In 2003, radio personality Krista Tippett launched a show called *Speaking of Faith*. It went fairly unnoticed until the popularity of podcasts grew, and it now has more than two hundred million downloads under the name *On Being*. Through that time, the data shows that the show bridged divides that had become increasingly wide in recent years. The listeners were diverse, crossing political, racial, and religious boundaries. Out of this recognition, *On Being* launched the Civil Conversations Project in 2011, which equips local communities with what they need to learn how to better disagree with one another and still be united as a community.[4] We have one in our area, led by my good friend Megan, and it continues to encourage me to see a future where love matters more. More than our political differences. More than our racial differences. More than our religious differences.

The fact that love matters more doesn't mean we get to ignore our differences. It doesn't mean our differences don't matter. Or that we shouldn't all be working together to acknowledge, and solve, the problems that face our society. On the contrary, because love matters more, we need to be more committed than ever to solving those problems. But I would argue that keeping love as the ultimate aim keeps us from tactics that undermine our ultimate aim. Keeping love as the ultimate aim keeps us from confusing our way with the best way.

Rather than ignoring the hard conversations about race, religion, and politics, we need to enter them, having built the right muscles: the right heart, mind-set, and disposition. I appreciate the six grounding virtues of the Civil Conversations Project:

- words that matter
- hospitality
- humility
- patience

- generous listening
- adventurous civility[5]

The heart of the challenge to let love matter more is to recognize that the presence of these virtues in our conversations, debates, and everyday life is just as important as what is said in these conversations and debates.

SPEAKING THE TRUTH IN LOVE LEADS TO MORE INCLUSION, NOT LESS

If we want to really get to the bottom of that phrase, "speaking the truth in love," we should probably get nerdy. So get out your Scofield Reference Bible and your Strong's Concordance, and let's do some good old-fashioned Bible study.

The question on the table is, "What exactly does Paul mean by 'the truth' when he mentions 'speaking the truth in love' in Ephesians 4?"

As your Bible study teacher, I have to say, "Let's first look at the context." If you're reading the New International Version, you can tell by the header that the context for Ephesians 4 is "Unity and Maturity in the Body of Christ." It is a sad irony that people use "speaking the truth" from this passage as a means to exclude. Paul begins the chapter this way:

> As a prisoner for the Lord, then, I urge you to live a life worthy of the calling you have received. Be completely humble and gentle; be patient, bearing with one another in love. Make every effort to keep the unity of the Spirit

through the bond of peace. There is one body and one Spirit, just as you were called to the one hope when you were called; one Lord, one faith, one baptism, one God and Father of all, who is over all and through all and in all.

Ephesians 4:1–6

If you notice, the phrase "in love" shows up here as well. So it makes sense that if you are "speaking the truth" to people in love, you are also "bearing with one another" in love. Those go hand in hand, but people who like to use the truth as a weapon conveniently tend to leave that part out.

So, whatever "speaking the truth in love" means, it can't be separated from these traits:

- being humble
- being gentle
- being patient
- bearing with one another
- making every effort to keep unity through the bond of peace

According to Paul, telling the truth cannot be separated from all these other things. So if we're not exhibiting all of these traits alongside our "truth telling," our words are invalid. If we are not walking in truth, what comes out of our mouths isn't authentic and isn't true in the biblical sense.

Given that Paul talks more often, more explicitly, and more emphatically about unity in his writings than about standing up for the truth, if we're picking and choosing which verses to prioritize in our systems of belief, I will go with "bearing with one another in love" over "speaking the truth in love."[6] Bearing with one another is just as much a part of love as speaking the truth. As we mentioned earlier, bearing with one another is a prerequisite for speaking the truth.

The next time we see this phrase "in love" is in verses 15 and 16—verses that include the one in which the popular phrase in question appears. I'll quote them together:

> Instead, speaking the truth *in love*, we will grow to become in every respect the mature body of him who is the head, that is, Christ. From him the whole body, joined and held together by every supporting ligament, grows and builds itself up *in love*, as each part does its work.
>
> *Ephesians 4:15–16, italics added*

So, whatever this "truth" is we need to speak, it is to be used to grow up into Christ to promote the body's growth in building itself up in love. Just as we mentioned in a previous chapter, it seems like the goal is to build up love.

Then to end the chapter, Paul gives instructions for what all of this means for our lives. It seems to me he is giving us the answer key to what all of this is about. It's not telling the "truth" in some abstract sense, but the truth about how Jesus wants us to love:

- Put away falsehood and speak the truth to your neighbors (4:25).
- Be angry, but don't sin in your anger (4:26).
- Thieves should give up stealing so they can work and give to the needy (4:28).

- Let no evil talk come out of your mouth, but only what builds others up (4:29).
- Get rid of all bitterness, wrath, slander, and malice (4:31).
- Be kind, compassionate, and forgiving (4:32).

As we saw before, truth in the Bible is almost always referring to honest speech or simply not lying. We see this here as well. So when the Bible in general says to "speak the truth," it's not saying, "Tell people your opinion," but rather, "Don't intentionally lie to people." So you're off the hook. Jesus won't judge you for not sharing your opinion about the sin you see in your friend's life. Just don't lie to them.

If your Christian friend comes to you and tells you he has decided to move in with his girlfriend and you think it's a bad idea, be thoughtful about how you talk to him. True love is probably not best expressed with, "Why would you do that? Don't you know that's a sin? I mean, do what you want, but I'm not sure if you're being a good witness."

Perhaps a better way might be, "You're moving in with your girlfriend? Tell me more—how did you two decide that?" If he doesn't ask for your opinion, perhaps the loving thing to do is not to give it to him unsolicited. Or perhaps another question is in order: "Can you help me understand how this decision squares with your beliefs as a Christian?" If he does eventually ask for your opinion, consider a response something like this: "To be honest, I'm not sure it's a good idea. My interpretation of the Bible says [*insert your convictions here*]. But maybe I'm wrong. Maybe we can talk more later? But listen, I want you to know I'm happy for you. Let me know when you need help moving so I can make sure to be there!"

Importantly, if our friends or family members aren't Christians, I suggest we follow Paul's example in 1 Corinthians 5 and be really cautious about when we insert our convictions. Paul says in verse 12, "What business is it of mine to judge those outside the church?" That's a rhetorical question by the way. The answer is "none." It is none of Paul's business.

Getting back to Ephesians 4, this is a pretty great list of practical ways to love people. All this talk about speaking the truth and being built up into Christ ends with a very practical list about how to love people. We see this over and over. If you pluck out a verse from the Bible, you can make it mean whatever you want. Some of us are afraid of getting our beliefs about God wrong. So we find verses that justify holding on to our beliefs with a closed fist. But if I zoom out and look at the broader context in Ephesians, I see that Paul isn't interested in holding to a long list of beliefs; he's interested in people who follow Jesus and his pattern of love. So, sure, tell people your convictions—just make sure to do it in the context of all these other loving traits, including bearing with them and not excluding them. In fact, if we were going to exclude anyone from our congregations, I'm guessing we should start with those who don't do these six things Paul notes in the last section of Ephesians 4. And strangely enough, being in a committed same-sex marriage isn't one of them.

I will not let people off the hook who feel they can separate truth from the Bible. When we do, we run the risk of committing the sin of Jonah—applying the verses that lead me to give myself and my tribe grace, while judging and excluding from God's grace those I disagree with or who make me uncomfortable. The real scandal of the biblical God is not who gets excluded but who gets included.

BEING NICE ISN'T THE SAME AS LOVE

Many words have been thrown around in this chapter that may give you the impression that "speaking the truth in love" is simply about being nicer. While I'm committed to the belief that we do need more compassion, empathy, kindness, and grace in our world, I also want to leave room for a different kind of love. Since love often resides in our actions as much as our words, love can also look like the scientist who spends most of her time in the lab to cure the latest diseases for the sake of humanity.

It's important to recognize that love takes on different appearances and that while we lack in some areas of love, we are contributing in many other important ways.

Another way to think about it is this:

- Some love by caring for the oppressed.
- Some love by breaking people out of oppression.
- Some love by fighting systems of oppression.
- We need them all.

For me, this means some have the gift of kindness and are best suited for caring for those who need to be cared for. Some have the gift of activism and bravery and are willing to be on the front lines and through gritted teeth say, like Moses, "Let my people go!" And there are some who are more timid but gifted with brilliance, finding strategies and tactics for fighting systems that break down love and health. Paul's advice comes to mind, which, interestingly enough, comes in the chapter just before his famous chapter on love:

Now about the gifts of the Spirit, brothers and sisters, I do not want you to be uninformed . . .

There are different kinds of gifts, but the same Spirit distributes them. There are different kinds of service, but the same Lord. There are different kinds of working, but in all of them and in everyone it is the same God at work. Now to each one the manifestation of the Spirit is given for the common good . . .

Just as a body, though one, has many parts, but all its many parts form one body, so it is with Christ . . .

Now if the foot should say, "Because I am not a hand, I do not belong to the body," it would not for that reason stop being part of the body. And if the ear should say, "Because I am not an eye, I do not belong to the body," it would not for that reason stop being part of the body . . .

Now you are the body of Christ, and each one of you is a part of it.

1 Corinthians 12:1, 4–7, 12, 15–16, 27

CHAPTER NINE

GIVING OUR OPINION IN LOVE

We have solved the problem of the tension between truth and love. There is no tension. The Bible does not talk about truth in some abstract sense of "beliefs and opinions" apart from actions that Jesus sums up as "love God and love neighbor."

But that doesn't solve the other practical question: "What about those people in our lives we truly do love—how do we tell them our opinion?" The key move here, of course, is that we don't call it telling them the truth; we call it telling them *our opinion*. That's an important example of the humility talked about in Ephesians.

About five years ago, we had a friend visit us from out of town. We had known her a long time, and she had visited us many times. This time felt different. She was a little more distracted and a little more distant. She got upset quickly and often, and she was getting defensive with our kids—which was completely out of character.

One morning, she'd had enough and with angry tears told me I had hurt her feelings. I immediately apologized, not even sure of what I might have said or done to hurt her feelings. I told her we should go get some drinks and talk more about what was going on.

She talked for a good two hours, and I came to the conclusion she was in a toxic and codependent relationship. Gulp.

I was at a crossroads. Should I tell her my opinion because I loved her and truly wanted her to be happy? Or should I keep my opinion to myself because I didn't want to risk the relationship if she disagreed with me or got defensive?

As the excellent book *Crucial Conversations* says, "The mistake most of us make in our crucial conversations is we believe that we have to choose between telling the truth and keeping a friend."[1] Of course, I would like us to substitute "my opinion" for "the truth" in that quote as a reminder to stay humble, but otherwise, I think that's some great insight.

It's easy to assume that this really is the choice we face. Most of us have stories of a conversation that has gone badly after we've tried to open up and give people "the hard truth." For some of us, if we're honest, it can be just as scary to give our opinions to others as it can be hurtful to receive other people's opinions about us.

I actually believe most people do want to hear our opinions. Most people don't want to be duped by their own delusions. They want to see things as they really are. However, the harsh reality is that most of us have a lot of insecurities that make us very sensitive to any information that shows us in any negative light. With that in mind, most people don't respond negatively to *what* we share but to *how* we share it.

Telling people our opinion *in love* takes more work than most of us are willing to put into relationships. So instead of doing that work, we often just blurt out our opinion whenever we feel like it (or when emotions are high and it just comes out of us) and then try to defend our statements with justifications like, "Well, I'm just telling the truth—it's not my fault people can't handle it." Or more often in our "polite" culture, we follow our parents' advice that "if you can't say something nice, don't say anything at all." That sounds good in theory, but it typically results in distance, where we just gradually disappear from relationships (what young people call ghosting). Rather than do the work of finding out the best way to share our opinions, we slowly disassociate with people who don't believe, act, or think just like we do.

In a world where we're afraid to talk to Uncle Frank at Thanksgiving about his politics because it will turn the entire meal into a passive-aggressive circus, telling people our opinion *in love* is a lost art—one we desperately need back.

Below are some practical tips as you work toward telling people your opinion in love.[2] Before we look at them, though, a brief disclaimer: I'm writing from my own perspective about times when we want to give people our opinion about what we perceive to be bad life choices. This isn't to say we should be okay with our voice not being heard. Or that we shouldn't put up boundaries with people who continue to dehumanize us in conversation. Many Christians, especially women, have been taught what might be called "doormat love"—that not being heard and getting stepped on again and again is a virtue. As if that's what being like Jesus is all about. This is simply a lie.

So know that each of these pieces of advice should be

filtered through the biblical wisdom tradition we find in the book of Proverbs: "It depends." On personality, circumstance, place in life, past experiences, mental health, and a host of other things. That being said, here are some things to think about.

KNOW YOUR HEART

The famed theologian of the sixteenth century John Calvin began his big book of understanding God (his systematic theology) in a curious way. In the first chapter of the first book, he made an interesting claim: In order to know yourself, you must know God. *And* in order to know God, you must know yourself.[3]

If John Calvin said it almost five hundred years ago in a widely influential book about God, and most secular psychologists affirm it today, then no matter how you slice it, it's important to be self-aware.

Full stop.

Just in general. In your life. Being self-aware is *essential* if you want people to feel loved when you share your convictions. Specifically, be aware of the feelings, opinions, and baggage you're bringing to the conversation. Be aware of what you actually want out of the conversation. We would like to think our motives are always pure, but that's simply not the case. Here's what I've found from doing this really poorly so many times:

Times I Know My Heart Is in the Wrong Place

Jared the martyr. There have been times in my life when I wanted the badge of "persecuted Christian," and since that was, if not my primary goal in a conversation, a nice consolation prize, I didn't really try too hard to soften how I was sharing my opinion. If these folks get mad at me for telling them "the truth," I'm being like Jesus—and that feels good. It feels even better when I get a sympathetic pat on the back from my Christian friends when I tell them what happened.

Jared the righteous. One time in college, a group of guys several dorm rooms down from me got into a theological debate (these break out like the plague in 1350 when you go to a Christian college). Then I heard someone yell, "Let's go get Jared." Yes, I was equally nerdy back then—and a lot more, um, how shall we say it, "competitive." They ran to my room and gave me the context of the argument, and I remember jumping up and jogging down the hall like I was freakin' Rocky.

The last thing on my mind that night was whether the people in that room felt loved. I wanted them to admire my smarts and know that I was right. It feels good to convince people you are right because it helps stuff down your own self-doubt. I have found the more important it is for me to convince someone else I'm right about something, the more I realize it's me I'm trying to convince. For me, when I enter a conversation feeling insecure or wanting to be right, it won't usually end with me loving the other person well.

Jared the savior. I am a recovering messiah. I like fixing things. I am a problem solver. It took me a long time to realize that going into conversations to fix people is often just as harmful as going into these conversations to be right. I can honestly attest to my pure motives for this one. I truly want to be helpful. But my need to be helpful will often outweigh the other person's need to be heard and loved. I am getting my emotional needs met by being the fixer rather than the lover. And those are two different roles.

Times I Know My Heart Is in the Right Place

- I want what is best for someone.
- I want someone to feel accepted for who they are.
- I want someone to feel heard.
- I want someone to know I'm sharing my opinion because I love them.
- I value my relationship with someone over getting them to agree with my opinion.
- I am willing to continue to be in relationship with them, even if they reject my opinion.
- I respect their choices as theirs to make.

This is a long list, and it's been a feat to get to this place with the people I love. But for me, that's the work of being a Christian. It's doing the work to love well.

CREATE CONDITIONS FOR SAFETY

If we are genuinely interested in telling someone our opinion in love, we not only must have the right motives; it's also important that the other person feels safe in our presence. Of course, this means physically safe, but it also means emotionally safe. If someone feels attacked, they will become defensive. If this happens, we should not feel offended. Our attempt to share our opinions about their choices has made them feel unsafe.

The road goes both ways. If you feel attacked or unsafe in a conversation, it isn't unloving to set up boundaries and not participate. Maybe you're being overly sensitive, and what they are saying is something you need to hear. Maybe you are being emotionally attacked and need to tell the other person you are feeling attacked, and then walk away. It's a judgment call you must make in the moment. This is why being self-aware is so important. Only you, through trial and error and growth in wisdom, can know where that line is for yourself.

I have found three important things to consider about creating conditions for safety in conversation: right time, right place, and right way.

1. Right time. It is not ideal to share your opinion when an emotionally charged conversation has just taken place. Sometimes that's the only time we feel courageous enough to say something—the adrenaline is pumping, so it feels like "now or never." If those are your only two options, choose never. Or better yet, go away from that conversation and write down what you want to say, shelve it for a day or two, and then come back to it, edit it, and set a time to meet and talk.

2. Right place. It may seem obvious, but it's probably not a good idea to give your criticism of someone's choices in front of other people. For most people, this is an unsafe place to either defend their choices or acknowledge that you are right. In my experience, these conversations best happen alone and in a neutral place.

3. Right way. The most important condition for safety is having the conversation in the right way. A few ideas are listed here, but this could be a whole book by itself.

- *Respect.* The wisdom of showing with your words and body language that the other person is worth your attention, time, and sincere engagement, regardless of your differences.

- *Active listening.* The wisdom of seeking to understand before being understood.
- *Curiosity.* The wisdom of wondering why, again and again, until you are interested instead of judgmental.
- *Humility.* The wisdom of apologizing when you've hurt someone or are wrong and of not apologizing when someone has hurt you or when you aren't wrong.

To summarize, we can simply point to bell hooks's list of what it means to love: showing care, affection, recognition, respect, commitment, trust, honesty, and open communication.

FOLLOW THE PLATINUM RULE

I once gave advice to two brothers who were not getting along. In their relationship, one of them found connection and intimacy through conflict. Getting into a heated discussion about their relationship with brutal honesty was the way to this man's heart. His brother was the opposite. He was so conflict-avoidant that if he was part of anything that smelled like a heated discussion, he started to retreat and disconnect from the person. For you Enneagram fans, one of the brothers was an 8, the other a 9.

So they had developed a deeply rooted pattern over the forty years of their relationship together: the more one dug in for relationship in the way that made sense to him, the more the other one retreated. And the retreat caused the first one to dig in even more, which caused the other to retreat even more. It was a vicious cycle that had turned ugly, even though both desperately wanted a healthy relationship with the other.

The problem? The Golden Rule: "Do to others what you would have them do to you" (Matthew 7:12).

You heard me right. The Golden Rule has its limits. Go back to the food analogy. What if I used the Golden Rule to feed my six-month-old baby and just gave him a beer and a bowl of spaghetti? I did to him what I would want him to do to me.

The Golden Rule is a good starting place. But without deep listening to the needs of another human being, we can find ourselves really hurting people with it.

That's why I endorse the Platinum Rule: "Do to others as I have learned from them they want done to them." They may very well thrive under an environment that I would suffer under. That's why true communication is at the heart of what it means to love. We love well when we understand who someone *is* and behave according to who they *are*. We do not love well when we behave according to who *we want* them to be or who we assume they are because of who we are.

It also goes back to one of the core principles of truth as freedom affirming: it treats people as adults who are responsible for their own choices. If you allow people to be people and not try to control them out of supposed "love" for them, you will learn how they want to be treated and then treat them accordingly.

WE LOVE WELL WHEN WE UNDERSTAND WHO SOMEONE IS AND BEHAVE ACCORDING TO WHO THEY ARE.

For me, the Bible is actually the foundation for all of this. The Bible gives us the trajectory, the tools, and the tether to come together and build a future that is faithful to the Christian tradition. It can't create the future for us because it was written in the past, but it can give us what we need, along with the Spirit of God in the here and now, to reimagine what it means to love like Jesus in the twenty-first century.

THE MESSINESS OF LOVE

I had to learn a lot of these lessons the hard way as a pastor. I was on a team of five pastors for a congregation of three thousand when I was twenty-four. That is young. Probably too young. The youth pastor was twenty years older than me. So, fortunately and unfortunately, being a pastor was a crash course for me in "speaking the truth in love." Emphasis on the *crash*.

There was a young woman in my congregation who was probably two or three years older than me and considered me her primary pastor. We'd had many conversations before. She trusted me, and I cared for her. She was dating someone she had met online, and he had recently proposed to her. She wanted me to officiate the wedding. According to our church's policy, that meant I needed to walk them through some premarital counseling before the wedding. He asked to speak with me and let me know that premarital counseling wasn't necessary and that they were fine. Yellow flag number one.

I insisted, and he finally agreed to a few sessions. It was clear in the first session that he was very uncomfortable—not in the normal, "Hey, this is awkward" kind of way, but in the "Hey, man, back off" kind of way. There were even a few questions where he responded with, "Why do you need to know that?" Yellow flag number two.

As I processed those few sessions, I became increasingly uncomfortable with their relationship. He seemed very controlling and also seemed to lack empathy. Of course, many of these experiences were new to me, so it took me weeks, probably months, to put the pieces together. All I knew in the beginning was that something was off. I went through all the stages of self-doubt: *Is this really a big deal? Is it really my business? I'm just officiating—what right do I have to get in the middle of things?*

I started wrestling with that question—*Can I tell the truth in love, or am I risking this relationship?* About eight weeks before the wedding, I knew what I had to do. I called the young woman and told her how I felt and that I was not comfortable moving forward with the wedding. Right time? Probably not. Right place? Probably not. However, I did my best to do it in the right way.

As I feared, she was defensive. She felt betrayed. She couldn't hear what I was saying. All she heard was that I wasn't willing to officiate the wedding. Sharing my opinion hurt her feelings in the moment, but I had checked my motives, and I knew it was the right thing. Within a year, unfortunately, my suspicions were confirmed. He was emotionally manipulative, controlling, and physically abusive. She had close friends who got her out of that situation. That was more than a decade ago. Our relationship was rocky for a while, but instead of saying, "I told you so," I said, "How can I help?" We are friends to this day, staying in touch and talking often. Love matters more.

The Bible was never intended to be a psychological manual

or an academic study of society and human relationships, *but it is a framework that can be expanded to include all of the knowledge we know now.* In other words, the Bible gives us this command: Love God. Love others. Love self.

What that means will change over time as the Spirit guides us into all the truth (John 16:13). The goal never changes. Love is still the goal. And in that way, we must always be faithful and tied, or tethered, to that trajectory of the Bible. But *what it means to love well* can and should change in each generation as we incorporate the God-given knowledge we acquire through scientific, historical, and theological study. And so where is the Bible in all of this? It's the necessary compost pile that provides all the nutrients we need to grow into a flourishing community that is faithful to the witness of those beautiful saints whose experiences are recorded in the Bible and in the rest of the history of the church.

But it is incredibly messy. The answer for when, and how, to tell people our opinion in love is not simple. Søren Kierkegaard put it this way:

> This is all I have known for certain, that God is love. Even if I have been mistaken on this or that point, God is nevertheless love. If I have made a mistake it will be plain enough; so I repent—and God is love. He is love, not he was love, nor, he will be love, oh no, even that future was too slow for me, he is love. Oh, how wonderful. Sometimes, perhaps, my repentance does not come at once, and so there is a future. But God keeps no person waiting, he is love. Like spring-water which keeps the same temperature summer and winter—so is God's love. His love is a spring that never runs dry.[4]

CHAPTER TEN

A MORE AUTHENTIC FAITH

My wife and I got married at age nineteen after having known each other for only thirteen months and after dating for eleven months. If it tells you anything, even our Christian college friends, many of whom went to college for the explicit purpose of getting married, thought we were rushing it.

DINNER THEATER

Within a few months of our wedding, we got an invitation from our friends to participate in a dinner theater experience. We had no real idea what that meant, but we signed up. It turns out it was a murder mystery where we all had to pretend to be a certain character all evening while also trying to figure out "whodunit." I learned something very important about my wife that night: she is a terrible actor.

Not like "haha, look at me, I'm so bad at this" terrible. More like "she left the apartment in tears about twenty minutes into the evening" terrible. I have since learned, over and over again, that my wife is built to be authentic. What you see is what you get. That night wasn't about ability; it was that she was being asked to do something she simply isn't built to do: pretend to be something she isn't.

There have been times when I wasn't really excited about this trait. If a friend offended her, she couldn't plaster on a fake smile when we saw them at the coffee shop. She wouldn't smile. She would be herself until they had a chance to resolve the problem. That could make things awkward for me at times. But my wife is built to be true to herself. She almost can't be physically or emotionally fake. And as I have matured, I've learned how amazing it is to be in relationship with someone who doesn't pretend.

If I'm honest, her authenticity offended me because it contradicted a belief I'd had since I was a kid: pretending so you can fit in is necessary to survive. Her authenticity triggered my deepest fear: that my true self wouldn't be accepted by my social groups. Her authenticity revealed my hypocrisy. Over time, though, my wife taught me the value of being true to ourselves, and my guard began to lower.

There is one place where the New Testament translates the word *truth* with a word we haven't talked about. In John 4, Jesus is talking to a Samaritan woman. They are having a friendly debate about whether the Jews or the Samaritans worship God correctly. Jesus had told her, "Yet a time is coming and has now come when the true worshipers will worship the Father in the Spirit and in truth, for they are the kind of worshipers the Father seeks. God is spirit, and his worshipers must worship in the Spirit and in truth" (John 4:23–24).

The word for *truth* here is a unique word. It's related to the word *aletheia*—the Greek word behind all of the examples we looked at in chapter 4. But this word is different. It's *alethinos*. It means "not fake"—it means "authentic." This is incredibly important in the shift we need to make as Christians today. For some reason, we've come to think that Christianity is about believing the right things. But true worship, as Jesus talks about here, isn't about worshiping God with right beliefs, but about worshiping God with no pretending.

JESUS AND THE HYPOCRITES

In fact, the way Matthew tells it, Jesus has almost nothing to say about people who believe the wrong things about God or the Bible, but he has a boatload to say about the dangers of trying to pretend to be something we aren't. The only true judgment Jesus doles out is for people with power who use rules and regulations to pretend they are purer so they can continue to control those without power.

Matthew uses the word *hypocrite* more than any other book in the New Testament.[1] It's such a loaded term today, but it simply comes from the Greek word for "actor." The first part, *hypo*, means "underneath" and was used because actors often used masks to portray different characters or emotions. So the actor would have been acting from "underneath" the mask. When Jesus calls out the pastors of his day, he is saying that they pretend to be something they are not. Then he gets specific: "Do not do what they do, for they do not practice what they preach. They tie up heavy, cumbersome loads and put them on other people's shoulders, but they themselves are not willing to lift a finger to move them" (Matthew 23:3–4).

This is a perfect example of what most people mean when

they talk about "speaking the truth in love"—it's truth telling without loving action. They arrogantly explain the rules to everyone else but won't get in the game. They put burdens of behavior on people's shoulders but aren't willing to bear those burdens together. They "should" all over people but aren't willing to pick up the shovel.

This is why it was so important in chapter 4 to realize the context for Paul's statement about "speaking the truth in love." Because without understanding what it means to be "in love," I cannot practice what I preach and I become a truth-telling hypocrite. Without love, the truth is not in us, no matter what we tell people.

Authenticity isn't too far off from how other parts of the New Testament talk about truth. As we saw in chapter 4, honesty and fair testimony are part of how the Bible describes walking in truth. *Fake* is another word for being dishonest or deceitful. Being fake is lying to people about who you truly are.

Jesus addresses the pastors and biblical scholars of his day with what is known as the Seven Woes. He begins the first one by saying, "Woe to you, teachers of the law and Pharisees, you hypocrites . . ." and then explains:

1. "You shut the door of the kingdom of heaven in people's faces. You yourselves do not enter, nor will you let those enter who are trying to" (23:13).
2. "You travel over land and sea to win a single convert, and when you have succeeded, you make them twice as much a child of hell as you are" (23:15).
3. "You say, 'If anyone swears by the temple, it means nothing; but anyone who swears by the gold of the temple is

bound by that oath.' You blind fools! Which is greater: the gold, or the temple that makes the gold sacred?" (23:16–17)

4. "You give a tenth of your spices . . . But you have neglected the more important matters of the law—justice, mercy and faithfulness" (23:23).

5. "You clean the outside of the cup and dish, but inside they are full of greed and self-indulgence" (23:25).

6. "You are like whitewashed tombs, which look beautiful on the outside but on the inside are full of the bones of the dead and everything unclean" (23:27).

7. "You build tombs for the prophets and decorate the graves of the righteous. And you say, 'If we had lived in the days of our ancestors, we would not have taken part with them in shedding the blood of the prophets'" (23:29–30).

Let me provide my best interpretation of these seven:

- You exclude people who want to be included.
- You care about conversion over character.
- You value the flash of gold over the simplicity of faithful practice.
- You follow legalistic rules but neglect what they point to: justice, mercy, and faithfulness.
- You pretend to be generous and self-sacrificing but are really greedy and self-indulgent.
- You are good at looking like life while inside you are dead.
- You celebrate those who spoke truth to power in the past while condemning those who are trying to do the same today.

Saying you are inclusive while actually excluding people, saying you care about character over numbers while building programs that are meant to grow numbers instead of character—this is what hypocrisy looks like for Jesus. It's the opposite of true love.

The religious leaders of Jesus' day were very good at "speaking the truth," but instead of being in love with their neighbor, they were in love with themselves. They were more motivated by protecting the benefits and control they had than by proclaiming that God had come to liberate with love. In that way they were not living truthfully but living falsely. They were not walking in truth, as John commands, but were walking in darkness.

What would it look like to reverse what Jesus pointed out about the religious leaders of his day?

- You include people who want to be included.
- You care about character over conversion.
- You value faithful practice over money.
- You pay most attention to justice, mercy, and faithfulness and think of rules as secondary.
- You admit when you are greedy and self-indulgent.
- You admit when you are dead inside.
- You celebrate those working for justice, mercy, and faithfulness, even if they step on your power.

TOWARD LOVING AUTHENTICITY

There's someone I have spent the past few years coaching who cares about authenticity above all. The problem is, he can be a real jerk sometimes—a title he readily accepts. We have spent a number of hours talking about this tension, asking the question, "Does authenticity mean you can be a jerk?"

We want people to be who they truly are. We respect and applaud authenticity. But what if someone is, by their own admission, a jerk? They don't try to hide it. They value authenticity above all else, and so virtue is *them being themselves*, even if *themselves* are pretty selfish.

To put it another way, "being true to ourselves" is messy. It's always wrestling between being and becoming, between who we are and who we want to be. It's accepting ourselves exactly as we are and yet acknowledging to ourselves and others that we haven't yet arrived. It's actually a pretty tricky tightrope to walk.

"BEING TRUE TO OURSELVES" IS MESSY. IT'S ALWAYS WRESTLING BETWEEN BEING AND BECOMING, BETWEEN WHO WE ARE AND WHO WE WANT TO BE.

Whatever we mean by authenticity and being true to ourselves, it begins with recognizing that we all wear a mask and that our preoccupation with keeping the mask pretty distracts us from the real work of becoming the kind of person we want to be. In other words, if I'm really interested in truth, I have to start telling the truth to myself about myself.

Many of us have gotten really good at telling other people the truth and really bad at telling ourselves the truth. This, Jesus says, is exactly the problem with the Pharisees. I don't think most of us got this way because we have the heart of Cersei and are after the Iron Throne. Instead, I think it's a culture we have built up in the church over the last several decades. And frankly, it's easier. It's easier to tell people where they are messing up. It's easier to pretend that we have it all together. But that's not walking in the truth: "If we claim to be without sin, we deceive ourselves and the truth is not in us" (1 John 1:8). Being authentic should not be an excuse to lack empathy, kindness, and compassion.

This tension goes both ways. Some of us have a harder time being kind to ourselves, even though we are kind to others. In other words, some of us are better at telling truths of grace and kindness to others than to ourselves. This is also a kind of hypocrisy. It might not be as damaging to others, but it is damaging to us.

In my late twenties, I lost my job as a teaching pastor of that large church near Philadelphia. The thought had never occurred to me that I might not be a pastor for the rest of my life. In fact, it seems my education made that almost a certainty. After all, what does an almost thirty-year-old with a degree in philosophy, another in religion, and three kids under the age of three do except teach and pastor?

Well, in my case, a few friends and I started a company. With no prior background or training, we began a marketing company that consulted and built brands, websites, and brochures. Within a few months, I found myself in rooms filled with marketing directors and marketing teams. And they were staring at me, waiting for me to teach them how to take their marketing to the next level. We continued to grow the company, and eventually I found my confidence. But for those first several months, I was almost in a panic every time I had to go visit a client. I was sure I was going to be exposed for what I was—a fraud.

It turns out I was a good consultant and I'm not sure I actually ever gave anyone bad advice. I knew what I was doing, but since I didn't have the experience or the degrees, I assumed everyone knew more than me. Even after a few years of success, I still had the feeling that one day someone was going to find out. There's a psychological term for this: imposter syndrome.

It's the feeling that everyone in a group knows more than me and that I am one mistake away from being exposed and told that my being in their lives was a big mistake. There are so many Christians who feel imposter syndrome every Sunday. The pastor presents an ideal way of life that seems unrealistic and out of reach, but as I look around and see everyone else staying calm and nodding their heads, I assume I'm the only one who can't keep up. I must be broken. I must be worse off than everyone else. And my deepest fears are confirmed: I'm beyond help, and once everyone finds out, I'll be kicked out.

Imposter syndrome. We begin to pretend. We put on a mask and learn the right things to say and the right things to do in public so that everyone thinks we're a good Christian. We pray every day that no one finds out the truth. Sound familiar?

This was me for many years. I worked so hard for so long on that mask of mine. I often had the prettiest mask, and it was seamless. Even if you looked really close, you couldn't tell it was a mask. Honestly, I had convinced myself it wasn't a mask at all. That's how you have the best mask, by the way. You have to fool yourself. If you can do that, the rest is pretty easy.

The problem was, I had spent so many years working on my mask that I hadn't really done much work on my true self. It's like those guys at the gym who spend all their energy buying all the right gear, making sure their hair looks decent, and making all the right moves so that people think they belong at the gym. They make it look so effortless. They're so busy with the superficial that they aren't building any real muscle. They're building the "pretend muscle." And some people get so good at building the "pretend muscle" that you wouldn't even know the difference.

Swap the gym for the church, and I see myself and the Christian culture I grew up in. I see a group of people who assume everyone around them are moral people who spend all their time reading the Bible and living like Jesus, and so they feel like frauds and imposters. And since we want to belong, and no one wants to be outed as an imposter, we begin to pretend. We spend so much energy on pretending, spending more and more time working on our masks and less and less time working on our true selves. Pretty soon, we don't even know the difference anymore.

The vicious part of this cycle is that the more we pretend, the more we convince ourselves that our true selves won't be accepted. And frankly, given how our female, divorced, and LGBTQ brothers and sisters have been treated over the past fifty years, we might not be wrong. This process of learning how to be true to ourselves and to others can be incredibly painful, since most of our churches are built for pretending.

I am convinced that for this kind of hypocrisy, the antidote is *vulnerable transparency.* It's a slow and painful process of taking off the mask and seeing how ugly we might have gotten because we've neglected the "more important matters of the law" (Matthew 23:23).

It was painful when I realized how much pretending I had been doing. I had to face the fact that I wasn't as good as I thought; I wasn't as loving as I wanted to be; I wasn't as Christlike as the mask I had worked so hard to craft was trying to convey. As Richard Rohr says, "Yes, 'the truth will set you free' as Jesus says (John 8:32), but first it tends to make you miserable."[2]

That was also the first day I realized God wasn't going to strike me down for having faults. As I peeled back the layers, I began to realize that *this* is what grace means. It means that God is a place of radical acceptance. And that led me to start finding other communities that showed the same radical acceptance. Not because I wanted to stay the same as I was and live in my faults, but precisely because I didn't. Remember the change paradox? It's not judgment that leads to change but acceptance. This is the heart of what it means to say that love matters more. It matters more than our faults. It matters more than trying to gatekeep our communities. It matters more than policing other people's behavior.

WHO WE ARE BECOMING

Authenticity, being true to ourselves, isn't the final destination. But it's a critical step. As we saw in Jesus' list above, there's more to walking in the truth than just authenticity. True love requires change, not just acknowledging our moral failings and character flaws. It focuses on who we are becoming.

What would it have looked like for the Pharisees to *become* authentic? Does it just mean they say, "You're right. We are greedy, self-indulgent, and dead inside. Whew, I feel better. Thanks for pushing us to start being our authentic selves"?

Being true to yourself only goes so far if "yourself" is a jerk.

As we've said, authenticity is about being honest about ourselves and charting a new path of growth based on what we learn. This how we learn who we are becoming. The real question is: "How close is our real self to the self we want to be?"[3]

For Christians, then, being true to ourselves is a two-step process:

- How close is who we want to be to the model of love we see in Jesus?
- How close is our real, everyday self to who we want to be?

Or, more simply put, Is my love toward God, others, and myself in proper relationship?

These are moving targets. Our vision for love enlarges when we learn something new about Jesus or have an experience with another human being. This is not a static set of rules. Moving from true beliefs to true love means moving from a formula for how to get it right to a messy, nonlinear process of figuring out how to love like Jesus. And that messy, nonlinear process is what we call "wisdom."

Some may say, "But what about people who don't want to be loving?" The short answer is, "I'm not worried about them. I'm not in the business of changing hearts." That's where we have to trust the Spirit of God and the Jesus Paul talks about when he says, "He who began a good work in you will carry it on to completion until the day of Christ Jesus" (Philippians 1:6).

The journey toward loving authenticity isn't to be policed. It isn't to be regulated. The show *Queer Eye* is a good example of this trust in God, this notion that true love begins with acceptance and respect and only then can opinions and feedback be given. There is a beautiful story in the second season. A woman who is respected in her church has a gay son. She is uncomfortable and spends a few years hiding behind the "truth" before realizing that her call is to love. Full stop. It is not to judge. It is not to give her opinion. It is to walk in the truth. She apologizes to her son for her lack of love and then stands up in front of her congregation and asks them to do the same.

It's time to stop pretending with each other. Our churches have perpetuated hypocrisy in the name of truth. Our churches have not been safe places for sinners—which, by the way, includes all of us. If you have moved to a place where you do not sin or do not even love and make excuses for your sin, then you do not have a broad enough view of sin. You have gerrymandered the lines of sin so that you are inside and certain people are outside. I would argue that you have made light of sin and have completely gotten wrong how we might overcome our weaknesses and failures.

The way is not through guilt, shame, or exclusion; it is through affirmation, celebration, and inclusion. We need to trust that the Spirit of God is in control, not us. We need to find our way to places where vulnerable transparency is celebrated as a step toward true love and not viewed as an affront to the rules and regulations that keep everything in its proper place. We need a place where there is no judgment but where there is repentance, where there is no punishment but where there is forgiveness.

Speaking the truth in love, then, becomes an exercise in helping people be honest about the gap between who they are and who they want to be, wrestling in community with how

God may not be calling all of us to be the same. And then we can walk arm in arm with them into their fullest potential, trusting that "he who began a good work in you will carry it on to completion until the day of Christ Jesus." In other words, churches need to be places where we can grow in Christlike wisdom.

CHAPTER ELEVEN

LOVE MATTERS MORE

There are some strange laws in Leviticus 19. But there are some great instructions in Leviticus 19 as well. Things like, "When a foreigner resides among you in your land, do not mistreat them. The foreigner residing among you must be treated as your native-born. Love them as yourself, for you were foreigners in Egypt. I am the LORD your God" (Leviticus 19:33–34), and "Do not seek revenge or bear a grudge against anyone among your people, but love your neighbor as yourself. I am the LORD" (Leviticus 19:18).

There's a story in the Bible where Jesus asks a Bible scholar how he thinks a person inherits eternal life. He asks him, "What is written in the Law? . . . How do you read it?" (Luke 10:26). The scholar says, "'Love the Lord your God with all your heart and with all your soul and with all your strength and with all your mind'; and, 'Love your neighbor as yourself.'" He has read his Leviticus 19.

He knows the truth. But like a lot of religious people I know, he "wanted to justify himself, so he asked Jesus, 'And who is my neighbor?'" Jesus famously responded with the parable of the good Samaritan (Luke 10:25–37), where a Samaritan, a member of a despised people group in Jesus' day, is deemed to be the one who has loved his neighbor as himself.

This story is a revolution on many levels. Jesus changes the meaning of Leviticus 19 to include non-Israelites. We are not called to love only those within our tribe, people who think like us and act like us, but we are neighbors with even those we hate and those who hate us. When we use *standing up for truth* to excuse our rudeness, our judgment, our feeling of discomfort toward people who aren't like us, we condemn ourselves as Bible scholars who "want to justify ourselves." And Jesus responds by pointing us to this parable that teaches us to love our neighbors, concluding with these words: "Go and do likewise" (Luke 10:37).

MUSLIMS LOVE THEIR NEIGHBORS

The most scandalous part of the parable of the good Samaritan is that if "loving your neighbor as yourself" is what it takes to inherit eternal life, it turns out that the Samaritan—a person considered by Jews to be a false worshiper of God—is the one on the right path. What was important wasn't the Bible scholar's knowledge but his *heart*—he wanted to use his smarts to justify his unloving actions toward those who weren't like him, and Jesus scandalizes him.

In December 2015, a bus was traveling from Nairobi to Mandera in Kenya. Somewhere along the way, it came to an abrupt stop when heavily armed members of al-Shabab, an Islamic extremist group, created a barrier. They forced everyone off and told them to separate by religion—Muslims to one side and Christians to the other. The Muslims on board knew what would happen if they separated from the Christians: the Christians would all be shot. Salah Farah, one of the men on the bus, recounted the event: "They told us if you are a Muslim, we are safe." But instead of choosing safety, they chose love. They refused to separate. Farah said, "We asked them to kill all of us or leave us alone."

Eventually, the extremists left in frustration, but not before firing several rounds. One of those bullets hit Salah Farah, and he died a month later in the hospital. But before he died, he told a reporter, "We are brothers. It's only the religion that is the difference, so I ask my brother Muslims to take care of the Christians so that the Christians also take care of us . . . and let us help one another and let us live together peacefully."[1]

Who is my neighbor? Salah Farah was the neighbor of that bus full of Christians he saved. There is no tension between truth and love. Yes, truth matters. And love always matters more.

"I NEED TO STAND AND FIGHT FOR HIM LIKE MY HAIR IS ON FIRE!"

Sara Cunningham is a Christian who was going about her business as a mom and wife when her son told her at age ten, "I'm gay." She dismissed it as the normal questioning of boys coming of age. He'd grow out of it. When her son, Parker, was seventeen, he told her again. She couldn't hear it. Here are some of her memories from that conversation:

I yelled at him, "You shouldn't even be thinking about this stuff!" . . .

He responded, "This isn't about sex, Mom! It's about me and what's in my head, who I am as a person. Being gay doesn't change who I am, or what I believe . . ."

I screamed at Parker, "JUST DON'T BE GAY!"

With his fist held tight, he stood up tall and yelled back at me, "I TRIED NOT TO BE! I AM TRYING NOT TO BE! I. AM. TRRYING. NNOT. TO!"

We stood there like prisoners in the spare bedroom.[2]

Her experience with her church during this time was hurtful. She says,

Hate the sin, love the sinner sounds real good if you're on the loving end of that equation, but if you're on the sinner's side of that prayer it feels dehumanizing and condescending or at least it did to me. All of a sudden, my son was the outcast stuck in a perpetual state of sin condemned to hell . . .

I was in my own private hell, certain the discouragement was growing inside of me like a cancer. I was torn between my love for him and this idea that he was going against everything holy. How could I accept something about him that the church, friends, and some family found morally wrong? I knew that I did not want to alienate Parker and if I could not change him, I was desperate to find a way to understand and accept him and even more desperate to resolve the spiritual conflict in my mind . . .

At night I would plead with God for an answer.

I was sick and tired of the confusion I had between God's grace and the message of condemnation from the church. DOES THE BLOOD OF JESUS CHRIST COVER IT OR NOT? . . .

I would pray: Give to it me straight, God . . . IF IT'S TRUE THAT PARKER IS GOING TO HELL FOR BEING GAY, THEN I NEED TO STAND AND FIGHT FOR HIM LIKE MY HAIR IS ON FIRE! AND IF IT'S NOT . . . THEN . . . well if it's not . . . I need to settle the hell down.[3]

At one point, when her son was getting married, she came down with an overwhelming sense of dread. She found herself in her laundry room in a conversation with God:

ME: God, I don't think I can handle any of this.
GOD: Girl, you got this.
ME: What do I do?
GOD: Celebrate Parker.
ME: How do I do that?
GOD: Love what he loves.[4]

So in 2015, she attended a pride parade wearing a pin that read, "Free Mom Hugs." She recounts, "Anyone who made eye contact with me, I'd say, 'Can I offer you a free mom hug or high five?' And I went home with glitter all over me."[5] From this small act, she began attending weddings as a "substitute mom" when parents of LGBTQ people refused to attend their own children's wedding. From there she founded a nonprofit called Free Mom Hugs that offers acceptance and support for the LGBTQ community, many of whom have been shunned and kicked out of their own homes or families.

Sara struggled. She struggled with the truth. She struggled with judgment and condemnation. While her struggle was about her son being gay, I see it as representative of how we respond to anyone we feel isn't behaving up to "God's standards." For us parents, our kids will make so many choices we feel aren't what's best for them. We may consider some of what they do to be "sinful" according to our beliefs. But beliefs aren't what we are charged with pursuing. All the Law and the Prophets do not hang on calling out people's sins in the name of standing up for the truth. Jesus says that literally nowhere. All the Law and the Prophets hang on loving God and loving our neighbor as ourselves (Matthew 22:40). And who is my neighbor?

OVERWHELMINGLY THE BIBLE SUPPORTS THE IDEA THAT WE SPEAK THE TRUTH BY OUR LOVE. IF WE WANT TO FOLLOW JESUS, LOVE WILL NEED TO BE OUR GUIDE.

Some may say this level of acceptance for people is modern, a way of compromising with contemporary culture. But I'm with Saint Ignatius Brianchaninov, a nineteenth-century Orthodox monk, who said, "Whatever you do, on no account condemn anyone; do not even try to judge whether a person is good or bad, but keep your eyes on that one evil person for whom you must give an account before God—yourself."[6]

If our response to Sara's story is, "Yeah, but don't we need to stand up for the truth?" then perhaps we are still slaves to the idol of truth. Overwhelmingly the Bible supports the idea that we speak the truth *by* our love. If we want to follow Jesus, love will need to be our guide. I know it's risky. But whoever said Christianity was safe? Love is always risky. Even if we wrestle away from our dependency on beliefs that are solely in our heads to help us feel like good Christians, we will still need to wrestle, likely for the rest of our lives, with love.

COUP CLUTZ CLOWNS

There has been a lot of news coverage about the rise of white supremacists and other racist groups. In 2017, a "Unite the Right" rally in Charlottesville, Virginia, turned violent, with twenty-eight injured and one dead, when James Alex Fields Jr. deliberately rammed his car into a crowd of protesters. It turned out that thousands had shown up to protest the rally, which ended up having only twenty to thirty actual participants.

One of my favorite stories of treating our enemies with love comes from another white supremacist rally held in a park in downtown Knoxville, Tennessee, on May 26, 2007. Just like in Charlottesville, this rally attracted about thirty supporters and about sixty people who wanted to protest the rally. Rather than turning violent, these protesters used a different tactic. They showed up as the Coup Clutz Clowns, a troupe of clowns who marched into the rally on stilts and unicycles, complete with clown makeup, colorful wigs, and red noses. They pretended to be in favor of the rally but kept misunderstanding the chant "White Power."

First, they thought people were chanting "White Flour," so the clowns proceeded to pull out bags of flour and playfully throw fistfuls of the flour at each other. The attention quickly turned from the rally itself to the wonderful spectacle of these clowns. One of the clowns then pointed out that they had been getting it wrong and suggested it was "White Flowers," so they all began to chant "White Flowers" while running around to give everyone they met a white flower.

And on it went, from "White Flower" to "Tight Shower" and ending with another group of clowns dressed in wedding dresses, yelling "Wife Power." It disrupted the rally and refocused the attention of the day on fun, connection, and love.[7]

It was so impactful that someone wrote the story as a children's book, titled *White Flour*. The author, David LaMotte, also wrote a poem about the experience, which ends with these words:

> *And what would be the lesson of that shiny*
> *southern day?*
> *Can we understand the message that the clowns*
> *sought to convey?*
> *Seems that when you're fighting hatred, hatred's not*
> *the thing to use!*
> *So here's to those who march on in their big red*
> *floppy shoes.*[8]

I really like this story for so many reasons, but the main reason may not be obvious. It's that love takes work. Responding to hatred with hatred is easy. But finding ways to love the oppressed and marginalized without resorting to hatred for the oppressor is harder than you might imagine. All the planning, the purpose, the shopping, the showing up. These clowns showed how, to paraphrase Dr. Martin Luther King's famous line, to drive out darkness with light and hate with love.[9] Or as Tim Keller once tweeted, "Tolerance isn't about not having beliefs. It's about how your beliefs lead you to treat people who disagree with you."[10]

True love is about how we treat people who disagree with us. Our love starts to crumble when we make truth an idol and use it to hide our disdain for our enemies, for those we disagree with, for those who aren't like us. As Jesus says in the Sermon on the Mount:

> "You have heard that it was said, 'Love your neighbor and hate your enemy.' But I tell you, love your enemies and pray for those who persecute you, that you may be children of your Father in heaven. He causes his sun to rise on the evil and the good, and sends rain on the righteous and the unrighteous. If you love those who love you, what reward will you get? Are not even the tax collectors doing that? And if you greet only your own people, what are you doing more than others? Do not even pagans do that?"
>
> *Matthew 5:43–47*

From God's perspective, from the perspective of love, someone watching you wouldn't know the difference between your neighbor and your enemy. Jesus doesn't say that God sends rain on the good people and withholds rain from the bad people because God "doesn't condone their lifestyle." It doesn't say that God keeps the sun from rising on those who make bad choices so that hopefully they'll repent.

"This can't be," you might say. "I mean, honestly, what would people from church think if God was seen being gracious and generous to people who were openly living in sin?" That's not what this passage says. It says there is no special God-calculus where we dole out our compassion, presence, acceptance, and love based on how well someone's life matches up to what we feel are godly standards. No, Jesus says that God followers love indiscriminately. Withholding love to show someone you love them is literally nonsense in the kingdom of God.

That's what I mean when I say that love matters more. I mean what you believe *doesn't matter* when it comes to love. I don't need to know what you believe or how you live your life to know it's my responsibility as a follower of Jesus to love you in such a way that others wouldn't know whether you're one of "my people" or "my enemy." When God is involved, the line between "us" and "them" gets blurry because when love matters more, the lines we have drawn get erased.

Another thing I don't see God doing is making sure we know all the places we fall short before God sends rain or sunshine on us. The gifts of God are given indiscriminately and without strings attached. That's what is so scandalous about the picture Jesus paints of God. Living a life of love patterned after Jesus, living a life of truth, isn't about telling people our opinions about their choices but about becoming "children of your Father in heaven," who doesn't tell people opinions but causes the sun to rise on the evil and the good, and sends rain on the righteous and the unrighteous.

When truth is our idol, we want to know what we believe

to make sure we are right and in the right camp. But when love matters more, we want to know what we believe to make sure we are falling more in love with people, which blurs the lines between our camps. As our friend Søren Kierkegaard writes:

> The task is not to find the lovable object, but to find the object before you lovable . . . and to be able to continue finding this one lovable, no matter how that person changes . . .
>
> We foolish people often think that when a person has changed for the worse, we are exempted from loving him . . . If this is how you see the person, then you really do not see him; you merely see unworthiness, imperfection, and admit thereby that when you loved him you did not really see *him* but saw only his excellence and perfections. True love is a matter of loving the very person you see. The emphasis is not on loving the perfections, but on loving the *person* you see, no matter what perfections or imperfections that person might possess.[11]

BACKSLIDING TOWARD LOVE

When I was a pastor, I started having doubts about the list of things I believed about God. I went from someone who "stood up for what I believed" to someone who more often than not shrugged my shoulders and said, "I don't know—that's a great question." This was a difficult time in my marriage. I distinctly remember a conversation my wife and I had in which she expressed her concerns.

We were sitting in the living room of our small apartment, with our two little boys sleeping upstairs, when she said, "What's been going on with you? You used to be so passionate about God, the Bible, and what you believe. You used to stand up for truth, and now you seem so wishy-washy."

This shook me. She was saying the very words I had heard growing up, directed at what we would call Christians who were "backsliding," who were starting to be lured by the comforts and wishy-washiness of the culture. Not only that, but she had told me that when we got married, there were two important things that attracted her to me: my faith and my confidence. Now it felt like both were on the line.

I didn't have an answer for her that night. But a few nights later, I was able to respond. I still remember what I said, almost word for word, because it began a journey that has led me to this very moment, writing this very paragraph:

> I want you to know I am still me. I have never been more passionate about God and the Bible than I am right now. But you're right, I am not interested in standing up for truth anymore. I am interested in standing up for love and for people. My love for the Bible has led me here. I don't think I'm compromising with the world, but I'm following what I see in the Bible.

Within a year, I had left my job as a pastor and started on this long and strange journey. It's been a journey away from hanging my faith on the certainty of my beliefs about God and a journey toward trusting God's love and exploring how best to forward that love to others.

ACKNOWLEDGMENTS

I'm incredibly grateful for everyone's support in writing this book. So many things had to fall into place to make it possible, and each required other people's time and energy. Thanks for letting me stand on your shoulders.

Pete Enns—your invitation to coauthor *Genesis for Normal People* in 2012 started a wonderful partnership that changed the trajectory of my life. You've been a good friend, a benevolent mentor in the world of writing, and a hyperanalytical pain in the neck. This book doesn't happen without you in the most concrete of ways.

Sarah—your support means the world to me. When I struggle with my passion to help others and the time it can take away from our family, you're always there to remind me we're in this together and we do it as a team. Your love frees me and holds me accountable, and for both, I'm grateful.

Salford Mennonite Church—our family journey with church has been bittersweet. Just when we were ready to give up, we found you. You're a bunch of imperfect people stumbling toward love together, built on three hundred years of tradition. Thank you for showing me what community can look like and for the hope you give me for the church of the future. Thanks to Foundations, the Sunday school class I have the honor of facilitating, for your patience as I tried out a few of these ideas on you the past few years.

The women in my family—Mom, Charissa, Aunt Carolyn, Aunt Barb—you all have what doctors call "strong personalities." Yet you don't let your strong opinions get in the way of relationship. You show up for each other. When it matters most and when it doesn't much matter at all. You show me what love looks like in the little nooks and crannies of life. You've been my loudest cheering section, and I do much of what I do to make you proud.

The team at The Bible for Normal People—Reed, Shay, and Megan—I always get queasy about self-promotion, but you've been so helpful and supportive in getting this book's message out there. I believe in it deeply, so to see you get behind it is uplifting and confidence-building.

The team at Zondervan—from the beginning, I've been up-front about needing to have my hand held through the publishing process, and you've delivered. Special thanks to Andy for being so available and gracious, to Dirk, and to Bridgette. You all get a gold star!

NOTES

Chapter 1: Only God Knows It's an Elephant

1. See Wikipedia's entry, "Blind Men and an Elephant," https://en.wikipedia.org/wiki/Blind_men_and_an_elephant.
2. See Dana Ford, "What Color Is This Dress?" *CNN*, February 27, 2015, www.cnn.com/2015/02/26/us/blue -black-white-gold-dress/index.html.
3. See Amanda Jackson, "Laurel or Yanny? What Science Has to Say," *CNN*, May 16, 2018, www.cnn.com/2018/05/15 /health/yanny-laurel-audio-social-media-trnd/index.html.
4. Juvenal, *Juvenal and Persius*, trans. George Gilbert Ramsay (New York: Putnam's Sons, 1918), 97, https://archive.org /details/juvenalpersiuswi00juveuoft/page/96.
5. See Wikipedia's entry, "Black Swan Emblems and Popular Culture," https://en.wikipedia.org/wiki/Black_swan _emblems_and_popular_culture.
6. In fact, statistician Nassim Nicholas Taleb published a book called *The Black Swan: The Impact of the Highly Improbable* (New York: Random House, 2007) to show how much we just don't know and how scientific methodologies are ill-equipped to predict these rare and

highly disruptive events in history, science, finance, and technology.

7. Brand Blanshard, *The Nature of Thought* (London: Allen & Unwin, 1939), 2:269.

Chapter 2: Truth Is Overworked and Underpaid

1. Richard Rorty, *Consequences of Pragmatism: Essays, 1972–1980* (Minneapolis: University of Minnesota Press, 1982), 166–67, italics original.

2. Referring, of course, to how we often mess up the first pancake because it's through the first pancake we figure out what we've done wrong (for example, need more flour; griddle is too hot, etc.).

3. Simon Blackburn, *On Truth* (New York: Oxford University Press, 2018), 34.

4. "The Word of the Year: 'Truthiness,'" *CBS News*, December 9, 2006, www.cbsnews.com/news/the-word-of -the-year-truthiness.

5. Oscar Wilde, *The Importance of Being Earnest* (1899; repr., New York: Dover, 2012), 6.

6. Cited in interview: "Kellyanne Conway: Press Secretary Sean Spicer Gave 'Alternative Facts,'" *Meet the Press: NBC News*, January 22, 2017, www.youtube.com/watch?v=VSr EEDQgFc8.

7. "Scientific Consensus: Earth's Climate Is Warming," NASA, https://climate.nasa.gov/scientific-consensus.

8. See Max Rappaport, "The Definitive History of 'Trust the Process,'" *Bleacher Report*, August 23, 2017, https:// bleacherreport.com/articles/2729018-the-definitive-history -of-trust-the-process.

9. See Max Roser, "Life Expectancy" (2019), https://ourworld indata.org/life-expectancy.

10. Jonathan Sacks, *The Great Partnership: Science, Religion, and the Search for Meaning* (New York: Schocken, 2011), 2, 6, italics original.

11. Speaking of truth, there has been debate on whether this was Gaiman or Chesterton who first quoted it. Gaiman cleared that up on his blog a number of years ago ("The sentiment is his. The phrasing is mine"), http://neil-gaiman .tumblr.com/post/42909304300/my-moms-a-librarian-and -planning-to-put-literary.

12. For the nerdiest among us, see Dmitry Leontiev, "Three Facets of Meaning," *Journal of Russian and East European Psychology* 43, no. 6 (November–December 2005): 45–72.

13. If you want to go down that rabbit hole and are up for a sophisticated philosophical look at the idea of "social construction," check out Ian Hacking's *The Social Construction of What?* (Cambridge, MA: Harvard University Press, 1999).

14. Augustine, *On Christian Doctrine, in Four Books,* Christian Classics Ethereal Library, 2.18.28, https://ccel.org /ccel/augustine/doctrine/doctrine.xix_1.html.

15. For those of you who are curious, let's clarify my heritage: my maternal great-grandmother was 100 percent Choctaw, my grandmother was mostly Choctaw, with a little Creek, and my dad was very much 100 percent white dude from Texas. My Mexican relatives referred to earlier are my cousins. My uncle married a Mexican woman. Whew, glad we got that cleared up!

16. "The Fox and the Grapes," in *The Aesop for Children* (Chicago: Rand McNally, 1919), 20.

17. "Foxes Eat Grapes," *Portland Guardian*, March 5, 1934, https://trove.nla.gov.au/newspaper/article/64285098.

18. Jon Elster, *Sour Grapes: Studies in the Subversion of Rationality* (Cambridge: Cambridge University Press, 1983), 110–42.

19. Philostratus, *Life of Apollonius of Tyana*, book 5:14, www .livius.org/sources/content/philostratus-life-of-apollonius /philostratus-life-of-apollonius-5.11-15.

20. For more on this way of reading the Bible, see my good friend Pete Enns's book *How the Bible Actually Works* (New York: HarperOne, 2019).

21. See Elizabeth Dias, ed., *What Did Jesus Ask? Christian Leaders Reflect on His Questions of Faith* (New York: Time Books, 2015).
22. Søren Kierkegaard, *Journals and Papers*, ed. and trans. Howard V. Hong and Edna H. Hong (Princeton, NJ: Princeton University Press, 1967–1978), 3:404.
23. bell hooks, *All about Love: New Visions* (New York: HarperPerennial, 2000), 4.
24. hooks, *All about Love*, 5.
25. Cynthia Bourgeault, *The Wisdom Jesus: Transforming Heart and Mind—A New Perspective on Christ and His Message* (Boston: Shambhala, 2008), 26.
26. "In Jesus everything hangs together around a single center of gravity, and you need to know what this center is before you can sense the subtle but cohesive power of the path he is laying out. What name might we give to this center? The apostle Paul suggests the word *kenosis*. In Greek the verb *kenosein* means 'to let go,' or 'to empty oneself'" (Bourgeault, *The Wisdom Jesus*, 63).

Chapter 3: Beware of Falling in Love with Cows

1. See the U.S. Department of Education's STEM page at www.ed.gov/stem.
2. Rodney C. Adkins, "America Desperately Needs More STEM Students. Here's How to Get Them," *Forbes*, July 9, 2012, www.forbes.com/sites/forbesleadershipforum/2012/07/09/america-desperately-needs-more-stem-students-heres-how-to-get-them.
3. For the nerdiest among us, check out how this was calculated at www.forbes.com/sites/michaelnoer/2012/04/23/how-much-is-a-dragon-worth-revisited.
4. Technically, it's "feeeeelllllliiiiiiings." They really don't like feelings apparently.
5. We'll talk later about how this can be taken advantage of too. Just as "speaking the truth in love" can be used as a

weapon, so can unlimited grace. I do not advocate being a
doormat for abuse and calling it love.

6. Carl Rogers, *On Becoming a Person: A Therapist's View of
Psychotherapy* (New York: Houghton Mifflin, 1961), 17.

7. By the way, King Jeroboam does the same thing a few
hundred years later in an attempt to not lose loyalty to his
rival in the south, King Rehoboam (see 1 Kings 12:28–29).

Chapter 4: Truth without Love Isn't True

1. R. Huna, quoted in the Babylonian Talmud, 'Abodah Zarah
17b, http://come-and-hear.com/zarah/zarah_17.html.

2. Shout out to all you DC Talk fans who just got that reference.

3. See John D. Harden and Marisa Iati, "How President
Obama Politicized the Use of 'Thoughts and Prayers' after
Mass Shootings," April 20, 2019, www.washingtonpost
.com/religion/how-president-obama-politicized-thoughts
-and-prayers after mass-shootings/2019/04/19/2895d7b6
-5d5c-11e9-a00e-050dc7b82693_story.html.

4. Sarah Faidell and Bex Wright, "New Zealand's Parliament
Voted 119–1 to Change Its Gun Laws, Less Than a Month
after Mass Shooting," April 10, 2019, www.cnn.com/2019
/04/10/asia/new-zealand-gun-law-reform-intl/index.html.

5. Søren Kierkegaard, *Provocations: Spiritual Writings of
Kierkegaard*, ed. Charles E. Moore (Farmington, PA:
Bruderhof Foundation, Inc., 2002), 66, italics original,
reprinted from www.bruderhof.com. Used with permission.

6. Søren Kierkgaard, *Practice in Christianity*, vol. 20 of
Kierkegaard's Writings, ed. Howard V. Hong and Edna H.
Hong (Princeton, NJ: Princeton University Press, 2013), 205.

7. Søren Kierkegaard, *The Concept of Anxiety*, ed. Alistair
Hannay (New York: Liveright, 2014), 166–67.

8. See, for example, 2 Timothy 2:15–18 and 2 Thessalonians
2:10–13.

9. Even if you take 2 Timothy 3:16 to be about the Bible in
general, it talks about the usefulness of the Bible. Many read

into the phrase "God-breathed" the assumption that we need to defend the accuracy of the Bible. But it's important to recognize that this would be an interpretation, not a conclusion that is obvious from that phrase.

10. One day when you're bored, see also Genesis 24:49; 32:10; 47:29; Exodus 34:6; 2 Chronicles 31:20; 32:1; Nehemiah 7:2; Psalms 25:10; 26:3; 30:9; Proverbs 3:3; Isaiah 16:5.

11. See also Genesis 42:16; Proverbs 12:19; 1 John 2:4.

12. See also Deuteronomy 13:14; 17:4; 22:20; 2 Chronicles 9:5; Zechariah 8:16.

13. bell hooks, *All about Love: New Visions* (New York: HarperPerennial, 2000), 4–5.

Chapter 5: If It Doesn't Set You Free, It's Not True

1. Maya Angelou, "Love Liberates," originally aired on *Oprah's Master Class* and transcribed from the podcast version of the interview found here: https://player.fm/series /oprahs-master-class-the-podcast/dr-maya-angelou.

2. Thich Nhat Hanh, *True Love: A Practice for Awakening the Heart*, trans. Sherab Chödzin Kohn (Boston: Shambhala, 2006), 4.

3. Søren Kierkegaard, *Works of Love: Some Christian Reflections in the Form of Discourses*, ed. Howard V. Hong and Edna H. Hong (Princeton, NJ: Princeton University Press, 1995), 217.

4. I wish I had more sophisticated examples for you, but if you expect anything other than Disney movie illustrations when you read a book written by someone with four children who are still twelve and under, that's really on you.

5. *Tangled*, directed by Nathan Greno and Byron Howard (2010; Burbank, CA: Walt Disney Pictures, 2011), DVD.

Chapter 6: The Importance of Weaving Flax into Tablecloths

1. Cited in Aaron Milavec, *Salvation Is from the Jews: Saving Grace in Judaism and Messianic Hope in Christianity* (Collegeville, MN: Liturgical, 2007), 39–40.

2. Karin Hedner Zetterholm, *Jewish Interpretation of the Bible: Ancient and Contemporary* (Minneapolis: Fortress, 2012), 6.
3. Something to consider: usually the people selling you on "the Bible can mean only one thing" are really just selling you on *their* way of reading the Bible and why you need to agree with *them*.
4. See Martin B. Copenhaver, *Jesus Is the Question: The 307 Questions Jesus Asked and the 3 He Answered* (Nashville: Abingdon, 2014), xviii.
5. John D. Caputo, *What Would Jesus Deconstruct? The Good News of Postmodernity for the Church* (Grand Rapids: Baker Academic, 2007), 83.
6. The fact that the historical prophet Jonah probably didn't get swallowed by a giant fish, especially considering that the author is clearly not trying to say this is a historical story, doesn't take a single thing away from the profound truth that if love can change God's mind about people, it must change ours too.

Chapter 7: Love Changes the Truth

1. For a taste of the arguments made earlier in my life, see this 1998 Southern Baptist article (Richard R. Melick Jr., "Women Pastors: What Does the Bible Teach?" *SBC Life*, May 1, 1998, www.sbclife.net/article/329/women-pastors -what-does-the-bible-teach).
2. See "U.S. Sees Dramatic Growth in Clergywomen over Two Decades," *Religion News Service*, October 9, 2018, https:// religionnews.com/2018/10/09/u-s-sees-dramatic-growth-in -clergywomen-over-two-decades.
3. See "Report Details Trends for U.S. Women Clergy," *Christian Century*, October 30, 2018, www.christian century.org/article/news/report-details-trends-us-women -clergy.
4. See "Statistics on Women in Ministry," Evangelical Alliance, July 2, 2012, www.eauk.org/church/research-and -statistics/women-in-ministry.cfm.

5. See Caryle Murphy, "Most U.S. Christian Groups Grow More Accepting of Homosexuality," Pew Research Center, December 18, 2015, www.pewresearch.org/fact-tank/2015 /12/18/most-u-s-christian-groups-grow-more-accepting -of-homosexuality.

6. See "Majority of Public Favors Same-Sex Marriage, but Divisions Persist," Pew Research Center, May 14, 2019, www.people-press.org/2019/05/14/majority-of-public-favors -same-sex-marriage-but-divisions-persist.

7. Read, for instance, Leviticus 11.

8. See, for instance, Simon LeVay, *Gay, Straight, and the Reason Why: The Science of Sexual Orientation* (Oxford: Oxford University Press); all of the studies referenced in the "Homosexuality and Psychology" entry on Wikipedia (https://en.wikipedia.org/wiki/Homosexuality_and_ psychology); and even the episodes of *The Bible for Normal People* podcast, with guests like Megan DeFranza, Austen Hartke, and Matthew Vines.

9. Lewis Carroll, *Through the Looking-Glass* (London: Macmillan, 1872), 124.

10. Hans-Georg Gadamer, *The Relevance of the Beautiful and Other Essays*, ed. Robert Bernasconi (Cambridge: Cambridge University Press, 1986), 132.

11. Joseph K. Gordon, *Divine Scripture in Human Understanding: A Systematic Theology of the Christian Bible* (Notre Dame, IN: University of Notre Dame Press, 2019), 263.

12. Quoted in "Great Quotes," World Jazz Scene, http://world jazzscene.com/wordpress/great-quotes.

13. That episode ("Interview with Jon D. Levenson: Resurrection in the Hebrew Bible") can be found here: https://peteenns.com/bfnp-podcast-episode-21-resurrection -hebrew-bible-jon-d-levenson.

14. Augustine, *On Christian Doctrine, in Four Books*, Christian Classics Ethereal Library, 1.36.40, www.ccel.org /ccel/augustine/doctrine.xxxvi.html.

15. John Craigie, "Dissect the Bird," from the album *Opening for Steinbeck (Live)*, March 16, 2018.
16. See the Pennsylvania Hospital website for more information at www.uphs.upenn.edu/paharc/tour/tour5.html.
17. Walter Brueggemann, *Texts under Negotiation: The Bible and Postmodern Imagination* (Minneapolis: Fortress, 1993), 61–62, italics original.

Chapter 8: Speaking the Truth in Love

1. "2019 Special Session of the General Conference, the United Methodist Church: Morning Session 2," February 26, 2019, YouTube video, 48:16, www.youtube.com /watch?v=_22cw_A2DOg.
2. Hayim Nahman Bialik and Yehoshua Hana Ravnitzky, eds., *The Book of Legends, Sefer Ha-Haggadah: Legends from the Talmud and Midrash* (New York: Schocken, 1992), 208.
3. Bruce Drake and Jocelyn Kiley, "Americans Say the Nation's Political Debate Has Grown More Toxic and 'Heated' Rhetoric Could Lead to Violence," Pew Research Center, July 18, 2019, www.pewresearch.org/fact-tank/2019/07/18 /americans-say-the-nations-political-debate has grown -more-toxic-and-heated-rhetoric-could-lead-to-violence.
4. To learn more or get involved, see "Civil Conversations Project," *On Being*, https://onbeing.org/civil-conversations -project. Also, consider the group Better Angels, which is also developing curriculum for how to talk across the political divide in a way that love matters more (see "Talking across the Political Divide," Better Angels, November 13, 2018, www.better-angels.org/talking-across-the-political-divide).
5. For a description of these virtues, see "The Grounding Virtues of the On Being Project," https://onbeing.org/civil -conversations-project/the-six-grounding-virtues-of-the-on -being-project.
6. See, for instance, Romans 12; 1 Corinthians 1; 12–13; Galatians 3; Ephesians 1–4; Philippians 2; Colossians 3.

Chapter 9: Giving Our Opinion in Love

1. Kerry Patterson, Joseph Grenny, Ron McMillan, and Al Switzler, *Crucial Conversations: Tools for Talking When Stakes Are High*, 2nd ed. (New York: McGraw-Hill, 2012), 22.
2. Some of these are adapted from Patterson et al., *Crucial Conversations*.
3. John Calvin, *Institutes of the Christian Religion*, ed. John T. McNeill (Philadelphia: Westminster, 1960), 1.1–2.
4. Søren Kierkegaard, *Provocations: Spiritual Writings of Kierkegaard*, ed. Charles E. Moore (Farmington, PA: Bruderhof Foundation, Inc., 2002), 302, reprinted from www.bruderhof.com. Used with permission.

Chapter 10: A More Authentic Faith

1. Again, when you're bored sometime, check out Matthew 6:2, 5, 16; 7:5; 15:7; 22:18; 23:13, 15, 23, 25, 27, 29; 24:51.
2. Richard Rohr, *Breathing Under Water: Spirituality and the Twelve Steps* (Cincinnati, OH: Saint Anthony Messenger, 2011), 30.
3. True love, by the way, is the space where that question is asked and allowed to be answered with no judgment, no expectation, no rush.

Chapter 11: Love Matters More

1. "Kenyan Muslim Who Shielded Christians in al-Shabab Attack Dies," *BBC News*, January 19, 2016, www.bbc.com /news/world-africa-35352763. For the original story on the attack, see "Kenyan Muslims Shield Christians in Mandera Bus Attack," *BBC News*, December 21, 2015, www.bbc .com/news/world-africa-35151967.
2. Sara Cunningham, *How We Sleep at Night: A Mother's Memoir* (North Charleston, SC: CreateSpace, 2014), 20–21.
3. Cunningham, *How We Sleep at Night*, 53, 57, 59–60.
4. Cunningham, *How We Sleep at Night*, 81.

5. Ariel Goronja, "Sara Cunningham: 5 Fast Facts You Need to Know," *Heavy*, July 25, 2018, https://heavy.com/news /2018/07/sara-cunningham.
6. St. Ignatius Brianchaninov, *The Arena: Guidelines for Spiritual and Monastic Life*, 2nd ed. (Jordanville, NY: Holy Trinity, 2012), 53.
7. See Sarah Freeman-Wolpert, "Why Nazis Are So Afraid of These Clowns," Waging Nonviolence, August 25, 2017, https://wagingnonviolence.org/2017/08/nazis-afraid-clowns.
8. David LaMotte, "White Flour," www.whiteflourbook.com /poem.
9. See Martin Luther King Jr., *Where Do We Go from Here? Chaos or Community* (Boston: Beacon, 2010), 67.
10. Tim Keller, Twitter post, July 15, 2019, 11:09 a.m., https:// twitter.com/timkellernyc/status/1150829633014784000.
11. Søren Kierkegaard, *Provocations: Spiritual Writings of Kierkegaard*, ed. Charles E. Moore (Farmington, PA: Bruderhof Foundation, Inc., 2002), 107–8, italics original, reprinted from www.bruderhof.com. Used with permission.

THE BIBLE
for Normal People

™

WE'RE CREATING CONVERSATIONS
ABOUT THE BIBLE ONLINE

The Bible For Normal People began as a podcast
to invite more and more people into conversation
about what the Bible is and what we should do with it.

In addition to the podcast,
we offer webinars, discussion groups,
live events, study guides, and more.

thebiblefornormalpeople.com

SUPPORT THE ONLY GOD-ORDAINED
PODCAST ON PATREON

PATREON.COM/THEBIBLEFORNORMALPEOPLE